Possibilities of the Impossible

Possibilities of the Impossible

Obstacles of Educational Reform, Nets, Trenches, Sinkholes, and Cisterns

Portia S. Bonner

ROWMAN & LITTLEFIELD
Lanham • Boulder • New York • London

Published by Rowman & Littlefield
An imprint of The Rowman & Littlefield Publishing Group, Inc.
4501 Forbes Boulevard, Suite 200, Lanham, Maryland 20706
www.rowman.com

86-90 Paul Street, London EC2A 4NE, United Kingdom

Copyright © 2022 by Portia S. Bonner

All rights reserved. No part of this book may be reproduced in any form or by any electronic or mechanical means, including information storage and retrieval systems, without written permission from the publisher, except by a reviewer who may quote passages in a review.

British Library Cataloguing in Publication Information Available

Library of Congress Cataloging-in-Publication Data Available

ISBN 9781475864212 (cloth) | ISBN 9781475864229 (pbk.) | ISBN 9781475864236 (epub)

Dedication
This book is dedicated to those who will heed the call of school leadership, take on the surmountable obstacles, and know that change is possible.

Contents

Preface　　xi

Acknowledgments　　xv

1　Leading Unwanted Change When Change Is Needed!　　1
　Section 1: Leading Change　　1
　Section 2: Rationale for Change Because Everyone
　　Is Not Achieving!　　7
　Section 3: What's Holding Us Down?　　8

PART 1: THE SETTING　　13

2　A Story of Three School Districts: The Setting　　15
　Section 1: District 1—Transitioning District　　16
　Section 2: District 2—The Shore　　17
　Section 3: District 3—Northwest　　17

PART 2: NETS　　19

3　Nets That Capture　　21
　Section 1: What's Captured Our Children?　　21
　Section 2: Institutional Structure and Tradition　　23
　Section 3: Leadership at the Helm　　24
　Section 4: Teachers' Collective Bargaining and the Rule to Work　　27

4　Nets That Hold　　33
　Section 1: Teachers' Expectation, Beliefs, and Mindsets　　33
　Section 2: Students' Cultural Diversity and Generational
　　Differences　　36

	Section 3: Parents' Involvement, Engagement, and Presence	38
	Section 4: Community of Have and Have Nots	41

PART 3: TRENCHES   47

5   The Trenches: Leadership and Reform Efforts   49
     Section 1: In the Trenches   49
     Section 2: The Board of Education and The Superintendent   51

6   The Trenches: More Important Relationships   59
     Section 1: Central Office and School Building Staff   59
     Section 2: Community, Parent, and School District   62
     Section 3: Policy Makers versus Systemic Institutionalization   64

PART 4: SINKHOLES   67

7   Sinkholes: Sustaining Reform Efforts during Political Tension   69
     Section 1: Sinkholes   69
     Section 2: Political Tide and Turnover in District Leadership   71

8   Economic Unpredictability and Funding   77

9   The Ever-Changing Pedagogical Approach   85
     Section 1: Pedagogy, Curriculum, and Assessment   85
     Section 2: School Safety, Climate, and Culture   90
     Section 3: Family Relationships and Partnerships   92
     Section 4: Technology: Blended Learning, STEM, and Personalized Learning   93

10   Accountability   95

PART 5: CISTERNS   99

11   Cisterns: Empty Wells That Are Not Being Replenished!   101
     Section 1: Cisterns   101
     Section 2: Teaching to the Middle and Lower Levels   102
     Section 3: Cultivating the Prison Pipeline   104

12   Workforce and Talent Development   109
     Section 1: Preparing Students for the Future   109
     Section 2: Globalization—Interdependent, Interconnected, and Competitive   113

PART 6: BREAKING AND FILLING — 119

13 Breaking the Nets, Filling the Trenches, Sinkholes, and Cisterns — 121
    Section 1: Visualizing the Perfect Educational Utopia — 121
    Section 2: Rigorous Curriculum Embedding
        Twenty-First-Century Skills — 122
    Section 3: Accountability — 124
    Section 4: Leadership — 125
    Section 5: Partnerships and Forward Thinking — 127

14 Overcoming the Hierarchy of Power — 133
    Section 1: What to Do? — 133
    Section 2: A House in Order Cannot Be Divided — 137

PART 7: DENOUEMENT — 141

15 Denouement: Overcoming Obstacles and the Possibilities
    That Prevail — 143
    Section 1: Entry into Superintendence — 143
    Section 2: Falling Short of the Right Fit — 148

16 What Do We Say? — 153

PART 8: DISTRICTS' RESPONSE TO ADDRESSING NETS, TRENCHES, SINKHOLES, AND CISTERNS — 159

17 District 1—Interweaving Coalitions and Strengthening
    the Mesh — 161

18 District 2—Embattlement of the Casted Net — 167

19 District 3—Building the Framework for a Strong Foundation — 173

20 Possibilities — 177
    Section 1: Moving Away from Traditionalism — 177
    Section 2: Improving Relationships through Communication — 179
    Section 3: Qualities of Future Leaders — 182
    Section 4: Revelation in the Metaphors — 185

Bibliography — 189

About the Author — 193

Preface

In a world with great technological advancement, the educational system still fails to equitably educate all children. This book is an eye-view account of experiences that provide evidence of obstacles that lead to failed reform efforts in school districts. In the first two chapters, I give a brief introduction of the metaphors used to describe barriers to educational reform and introduce three districts used as case studies to provide credence to such barriers.

In comparing the realities of how the educational system affects students, nets are the strongholds of a system that is no longer working; trenches denote broken relationships among stakeholders, leaving children stuck in the middle; sinkholes exemplify instability and unsustainability within the system; and cisterns characterize the preparedness of the next-generation workforce.

Nets have captured our children; trenches have caused division rather than collaboration; sinkholes have triggered instability; and cisterns mirror the holding back of student potential to achieve. The case studies support the stance of what is broken in our educational system. As the case studies metaphorically unravel their stories, it becomes relevantly clear that trusting relationships are pivotal for successful schools.

Possibilities of the Impossible provides metaphors of hindrances to educational reform using real-life case scenarios. A strategic way to describe problems is to paint a vivid image that lingers in one's mind. Such effects of the image make one rely on the details in its description, effects, and characteristics that give life to the image in telling a story.

Metaphors are good for describing situations by disclosing deep truths. I wrote this book to paint images that are indelible in one's mind of obstacles and that truly serve as barriers to substantial and successful reform in school systems. The book is written from the perspective of a superintendent who is leading unwanted change when change is needed at a period of time when educational reform is not addressing the needs of every child. Using metaphors of nets, trenches, sinkholes, and cisterns, this book shows instances of the obstacles that hinder academic success for our children.

The purpose of this book is to bring an awareness of what is broken in our educational system by looking at leadership and reform efforts in the midst of relationships, sustainability of reform efforts in economic unpredictability, the impact on the future workforce, and what is needed to overcome obstacles. A second purpose is to engage educators, in particular leadership, to think about how these obstacles impact their leadership efforts and the ability to build trusting relationships among stakeholders that is necessary for effective, transformative, and successful school districts.

Helping to prepare future district leaders to be forward thinking, they must be ready for the current and future state of affairs. Issues of trust, civility, political bravado, policies, funding, and the changing platform of teaching have always been issues at the forefront of schooling. But, as we become more self-centered and less caring about others as a nation, political will takes the mainstage of our decision-making. It distracts us from the focus on children and their needs. We are afraid to let go of tradition and fear the new as a means to dismantle the field of teaching, rather than embracing the possibilities of what could be.

The obstacles I discuss, in the form of metaphors, are a result of societal decay that impedes the achievement of children and the efficiency of the educational system. It paints a deeper picture of the oppressive injustices that are occurring within the educational system and why political reform efforts are adding to the barriers. My book points out that it is actually the relationships in which we fodder that determine the internal and external essence of the system that yields success for our students.

Sprawled throughout the book are also short vignettes and testimonials from leaders sharing their tales of leadership. At the end of each chapter, there are "Thought-Provoking Questions" (TPQ) designed to facilitate a deeper understanding of strong character traits leaders should bring to the table in order to navigate the obstacles that confront them in leadership. Each district case study, vignettes, and testimonials tell a story and give insight on strategies implemented to deal with the metaphorical entanglements.

This book is not intended to prescribe canned solutions to the systemic conditions in which we find the education system. It is the uniqueness of the culture, climate, and dynamics of relationships that steer which strategies are most impactful. However, the book is to encourage critical reflections of how a leader should prepare to address such issues as they engage the school district in change.

It is my hope that this book will contribute significantly to the establishment of trusting relationships that empower educational leaders to work through reform efforts for the good of their communities and help future leaders persevere and not fall into despair in their leadership journey, but instead learn along the way.

Acknowledgments

Thank you God for the words, experiences, and lessons.
Thank you family for your love and support.
Thank you Annie and Rena for being cheerleaders.
Thank you my superintendent friends for sharing testimonials.
Thank you Jill, Tom, and Jeanne for your commitment to children and the community.
Thank you Linda, Aresta, Lynnette, and Barbara for the many reflections over great meals.

Chapter 1

Leading Unwanted Change When Change Is Needed!

Institutions don't change only people change and in that, they change institutions.
—Bishop George Battle Jr, AMEZ Church
Former Board of Education Member

SECTION 1: LEADING CHANGE

Even though we have entered the twenty-first century, coined as the information age, we as a people have still failed to recognize the injustices or indifferences that occur within our schools. A far more superior age than the nineteenth and twentieth centuries, the twenty-first century's vastly changing technology, yielding more accessibility to information, whether factual or important, is driving most if not all of the innovative changes of the time.

However, when it comes to public education, innovation lags behind the fast pace of changing technology. There continues to be inequity and injustice in the arena of education such as the ineffectiveness of the public education system in preparing our children to be an active, competitive force in a global world that demands interdependency and interconnectedness.

Having the capacity for an individual to think critically, progressively, and creatively when solving problems and providing solutions that create useful resources for the future is pivotal for success in an ever-changing global environment. Some urban schools and districts have become tempestuous breeding grounds for destroying talent, potential, and dreams and have become celebratory in mediocrity by lowering expectations of students and supporting a need to maintain the status quo.

Rural districts are similar in fate to the inner city due to the poverty that resonates in small-town farmlands; the expectations that are held within these communities and what is valued are languid. Suburban districts, the stand-alones, are performing better on standardized tests and have a higher percentage of students entering college. But are students truly receiving a better education? Many suburban districts are witnessing transitions with their changing diversity of students and are not necessarily handling the change well.

Public education, a social experiment that John Dewey and Horace Mann would probably say, has pivoted in a negative direction resulting in predictability based upon demographic factors, expected bell curves, gaps, inadequacies, and inequities. Quantitatively speaking, the results of failing schools manifest themselves in the perpetuation of poor academic student achievement, high dropout rate, low graduation rate, and un-readiness for college and qualitatively yield underdeveloped students, who are poorly motivated or socially emotionally apathetic and displaying ever-increasing signs of hopelessness.

More recently, the increase in cases of inflating students' performance by cheating on standardized test,[1] over-testing of our students, suspicion of inflating scores, grade inflation, and/or weakening the difficulty of the test send a message that we have lost the purpose and value of a "good" education. What has gone wrong in an institution founded on the premises of securing a community's future by producing productive citizens that contribute to society?

This book is written from the perspective of an administrator serving in the capacity of superintendent of schools, one who has come up through the ranks serving as teacher, department and school administrator, to district-wide level. It is a reflection of experiences and testimonials of other leaders pointing out what is needed, recounting moments of hope for the educational system to redeem itself, and other moments that reveal the glaring realities of dysfunction. Realizing that for truly effective change to occur (and not change for the sake of changing), structures and systems have to be deconstructed and relationships have to be re-established that are respectful of each other's contributions.

Using metaphors of nets, trenches, sinkholes, and cisterns, this book uses comparisons to these structures to show instances of the obstacles that hinder academic success for our children. Nets are the strongholds of a system that are no longer working. Trenches denote broken relationships among stakeholders leaving children in the middle. Sinkholes exemplify instability and unsustainability within the system. Cisterns characterize the preparedness of the next-generation workforce.

> **TEXTBOX 1.1**
>
> Nets—Strongholds of a system that are no longer working.
> Trenches—Broken relationships among stakeholders.
> Sinkholes—Instability and unsustainability.
> Cisterns—Preparedness of the next generation.

As a figure of speech that makes implicit comparisons between two unrelated things, the choice of metaphors is used to create a visual and graphic image in one's mind that leads to a better understanding of the obstacles within the educational system. Although the metaphorical choices of nets, trenches, sinkholes, and cisterns are unrelated to the arena of education, there are common characteristics inherent in these structures that are telling. Each structure's functionality resembles the barriers to successful educational reform.

Using these four structures to paint a vivid image of these barriers hopefully creates powerful thoughts of innovation and evokes emotions around the need for change, challenging us to fix what is broken with the premise to illuminate the mind and to provide a deeper understanding of the surmountable problems in education and thinking about possible solutions.

These structures were selected not only for their uniqueness and affinity to water but because each is viewed as a containment structure, to hold, gather, hide, protect, store, or hold captive. Each of the four structures selected comparatively visualizes pivotal points about the obstacles we are contending with in education.

Although the structures are either used in water (nets), occur in water (trenches), are caused by moving water (sinkholes), or collect water (cistern), their various functions include provision, movement, and the availability of a resource necessary for life. Water is essential for life. Without it, we would die. It is life-giving flow that is necessary for every metabolic function in our bodies.

We can say the same for education and the need for knowledge to thrive. Education is the life force that is supplied through the institutionalized system of education. It is to provide an environment that is conducive for children to thrive, as they move through the grades and availability of opportunities for growth. Education in the Western culture is still considered to be a gateway to a better life; its attainment opens bigger and better doors to possibilities.

Nets, especially casting nets, are used to catch fish or bait in mass. We can corral the fish into the net and trap them in such a manner that there is nowhere else for the fish to go. Such control has the net that we can decide which fish stays in the net and those that are released. Rather than fish, we can refer to our children in the net. Many have limited choices and options of schooling and are trapped in the system that categorizes them into groups based upon prejudged and perceived expectations and demographic statistics.

Long, narrow, and sometimes deep depressions, that is, trenches, are found naturally along the seafloor. These types of trenches are caused by subduction, a force of one plate pushing against another, causing one to fold beneath another. These are the sites of seismic activity, that is, hotspots. Education systems are hot spots of much activity, but the product is questionable.

However, there is another type of trench that is used in warfare, also long, narrow, and sometimes deep. Such trenches are made by tunneling, sapping, or sandbagging (especially in high water table areas). Trenches such as these provide shelter for soldiers, a means to retrieve injured soldiers and sneak attacks over enemy lines. Trenches show extreme depth, naturally and logistically, in their construction. This metaphorical structure is used to describe the importance of trusting relationships within and among the hierarchical strata of the education system.

Sinkholes are caused by moving water with no surface access. And like trenches, they create depressions, but they have no natural external surface drainage. The sinkhole forms as a result of water seeping into the soil and subsurface. Amazing underground caverns and spaces form. When those underground spaces become too big, there is not enough support for the land above, then the spaces collapse forming a sinkhole.

Many of the nation's landfills covered with topsoil are at risk for such a catastrophe. Piling up our trash, trying to cover it up just to be exposed by a giant sinkhole, this structure is used to describe the sustainability of reform efforts during economic unpredictability, political tide, and teachers' pedagogy.

Cisterns are human-made containment receptacles used to naturally collect rainwater. If there was a drought, the cisterns would become empty. There are no underground connections as observed in wells; it is totally reliant on rainfall. In ancient times, cisterns that were no longer in use as water sources were sometimes used as prisons. Drought-affected and broken cisterns are compared to the systemic approach of teaching to the masses, cultivating a prison pipeline, preparation of students for tomorrow's workforce, and globalization that hinders students readiness for a productive and prosperous life.

In validating the comparisons, these metaphors create fluidity within the text portraying truths about the need for the resources the structure supplies and addressing barriers that the structures have become. Through understanding these comparisons, we can begin to reveal the impacts such obstacles have produced and suggest possible innovative solutions. Schools provide essential resources of knowledge, but there are associated destructive forces as well.

These four structures represent the destructive forces that are disrupting the educational system and impeding reform efforts: comparatively illustrating the captivity of being stuck in tradition and institutional structure; gaps in student achievement, challenges in cohesive relationships, effective leadership, academic expectations, and contending with demographic factors; economic disparity and uncertainty, pedagogy, and curriculum recycling; and cultivating the prison pipeline and failure to prepare students for their future world.

As a result of using these metaphors, we can garner a deeper understanding of the problems that plague us in education, make insightful changes that impact students, and address the problems through forward thinking. In other words, nets have captured our children, trenches have caused division rather than collaboration, sinkholes have triggered instability, and cisterns mirror the holding back of students' potential to achieve.

TEXTBOX 1.2

Identify a problem in education. What metaphors can you use to describe the problem to better understand the intricacies of it? Suggest innovative ways to resolve the problem.

The purpose of this book is to bring an awareness of what is broken in our educational system by looking at leadership and reform efforts in the midst of relationships; sustainability of reform efforts in economic unpredictability; the impact on the future workforce; and what is needed to overcome obstacles.

A second purpose is to engage educators, in particular leadership, to think about how these obstacles impact their leadership efforts and the ability to build trusting relationships among stakeholders that is necessary for effective, transformative, and successful school districts. The case studies, vignettes, and testimonials support the stance of what is broken in our educational system.

Each chapter ends with one or more thought-provoking questions (TPQ) designed to facilitate a deeper understanding of strong character traits leaders should bring to the table in order to navigate the obstacles that confront them in leadership.

Throughout the country, the public education system is a hierarchy of layers or strata that are connected and interact with one another. If you were to analyze the hierarchical structure of a school system, you would probably deconstruct it into seven interrelated strata. These strata would be both lineally and laterally connected explaining the key relationships that determine the effectiveness of schools. These seven interrelated strata include (1) the institutional structure of the organization as a whole, (2) the curriculum and its rigor, (3) the leadership, (4) the teacher, (5) the student, (6) the parent, and (7) the community and the media.

Relationships that are forged or the lack of bonds within relationships that are not forged via a partnership between and among these seven layers can help explain the ineffectualness of some schools. It is the interaction and intra-action of these strata that is pervious to school reform and student success.

What has become the goal of public education? Why do researchers, educators, and powerful businesses and corporations purport that reforming public education is like finding a miraculous anomaly. Suggesting that with all the right components, a school could be successful. Let us review the history of education and the paradigm shift of its purpose over the years. Over the years, schooling's purpose has been defined as:

- Instructing youth in religious doctrine
- Preparing the young to live in a democratic society
- Assimilating immigrants into the mainstream
- Preparing workers for industrialized twentieth-century workplace
- Preparing the young to be productive in the age of technology and information (twenty-first-century skills)
- Preparing the young to be globally interconnected and competitive
- Instilling the young to be lifelong learners
- Developing character (character education) and social-emotional learning
- Augmenting career and college readiness

The purpose of education has changed over the years, and the goals are redefined depending upon the apparent needs and trends of society. Larry Cuban (2012, 12) states that

> public schools seek to achieve social, political and economic goals while promising each student individual success. Most district and school goal statements include such familiar purposes as preparing students for economic self-sufficiency, fostering civic engagement in the community and promoting equal opportunity and individual wellbeing.

Education, although its purpose has dynamically shifted in focus over the years, the functionality of it remains in preparing students to interact in society.[2] Whether morally by building one's character and values or managing the social and emotional well-being in response to others—to creativity and productivity—this all leads back to preparing students to play a constructive role in a democratic society.

Even in the shift from a literate society of everyone learning to read and write to a functional literate person whose educational level is sufficient to function in modern society, we now see the continuous emergence to a learning society in which every aspect of the community is in partnership to promote a culture of learning. These shifts caused by trends in society require both a change in the approach in how educators instruct and students learn, and what is taught.

SECTION 2: RATIONALE FOR CHANGE BECAUSE EVERYONE IS NOT ACHIEVING!

Thanks to accountability, and educational reform efforts, we can analyze numerous data points such as graduation rate, absenteeism, dropout rate, discipline, performance on a standardized test, college readiness, and achievement gaps that show we are failing. Both quantitative and qualitative data provide strong evidence and an urgent reason for change.

Instead of facilitating reform, these efforts have placed more constraints on educators. We are bogged down with paperwork, cookie-cutter practices, and less creativity in pedagogy resulting in low morale. Students have lost sight of the purpose for learning, all for paying homage to successful performance on standardized test bringing glorification or dishonor to the district.

Educators should want every child to have an opportunity to be exposed to experiences that will help them to grow. We can neither limit children's potential nor can we know the expanse of their potential. However, we can feed and nurture them. It is time! America is losing its ground as we produce a product that is substandard.

More and more students are being promoted without being able to read and conduct simple mathematical functions. Our current and past performance on standardized test is subpar and shows an ever-widening achievement gap between ethnic groups and social-economic status. We manipulate the system to meet accountability standards which most times means lowering our expectation to meet a data point.

With a cattle prodding approach to herding students into a classroom, we seat them at individual desks to complete an assignment and assign students to the classroom based upon age appropriateness. Traditions such as keeping students until the 180 days are up before promoting (even if they have achieved standards earlier) or promoting a student who has met all requirements except in a core area, that is, mathematics or reading, with nothing in place to assist the student who is now behind the standards. This is creating a cycle of failure, and America's children are falling further, and further behind.

We are a model of compliance and complacency, an old factory model that no longer works. If we stepped back in time into a one-room school in the 1920s or earlier, in a rural community, we would see that schools did not look very different. Construction was limited to a four-walled structure that included windows, a door, and hopefully a potbelly stove to keep the structure warm during the cold months. Instructional equipment and resources simply included a chalkboard, desk, and primers.

A single teacher served in the capacity of building principal, guidance counselor, social worker, psychologist, security officer, secretary, and maintainer. She would be employed by federal or local funds; most times salary was offset with lodging at a local family's house. This teacher would teach multiple grades and ages within a single classroom, adapting, personalizing, and individualizing lessons to meet the needs of each child.

School day on average was from 9:00 am to 4:00 pm with a break for recess and an hour for lunch. Schools were designed to its simple function. After World War I and the conception of the automotive age, modes of transportation allowed for students to travel distances. This permitted for the consolidation of students creating larger schools with multiple classrooms in one building, and students were sorted by chronological age. People began to migrate to cities, closing many of the one-room classroom schools. Even with this evolutionary change, one-classroom schools still exist in the form of micro-schools but are few in number.

However, most of our schools moved from neighborhood schools that were community minded and personable to large complexes of efficiency. Placement of these large consolidated schools would sometimes be far away from the community in which the child resided.

SECTION 3: WHAT'S HOLDING US DOWN?

What's holding us down? What is preventing success for many of our children? Are we fixed in our premise of how to educate students? Is it truly a one size fits all? Is the old industrial model of how to run factories like schools limiting innovative ways of instructing students, treating every student the same—adequate versus equitable education, a factory model that is now obsolete? We have always done it this way, why change?

What is in place is no longer working and has not been working for a long time. What is frightening is that we are no longer meeting the needs of future workers. The products we are producing are obsolete. We need a new model for students, one that can inspire them to think creatively, problem-solve, and work independently as well as collaboratively.

Some thoughts as to what is holding us back! Let's answer the question, "What would be a great school?" That is a good place to start. A place where students want to attend! Citing the infamous slogan of sitcom Cheers, "Where everybody knows your name!" Safe, friendly, not overly crowded, diverse, and an environment where a child can grow!

Schools should be places where teachers, who are loving, kind, compassionate, and approachable, are there for the sole purpose of helping children to learn, grow, and add value to their lives. Instilling the thought that through educational experiences, a child's horizon broadens, expanding the opportunity for one to cultivate and live a "good" life that is meaningful. A place where leaders know both the academic and social-emotional needs of their children and use data as a measuring gauge to drive improvement. Where board members and the leadership can define the reality in which one leads.

Schools must become the place where the community places a high value on education, which is evident through funding, and understands the valuable relationship between education and economic development. In sum, we need safety, love, opportunity, valued relationships with trust, accountability, and financing.

Relationships, such as those between the board of education and superintendent, superintendent and staff, teacher and student, teacher and parent, teacher and school, and school and community, are critical for the smooth functioning of a school system. Within the educational system, relationships are tethered, as roles and responsibilities are no longer delineated but are muddled, micromanaged, and/or ethically faulty.

Even more so the structure of the school day and year, the curriculum and expectations of students, determination of what is important to know, skill versus content knowledge, the clientele makeup of the classroom, age, and developmental appropriateness of students to the subject are equally as important to affecting the success of schools. We are at a fixed point of complacency and mediocrity, held back by the mistrust and division in our relationships and the lack of intentional focus on common goals.

Metaphorical structures such as nets, trenches, sinkholes, and cisterns all function to contain, collect, or hold something. Public education as an institution and the systematic strata within are the very causes of the dysfunction. Using comparisons to these metaphorical structures demonstrates the disadvantages that occur when forces like this exist in education, resulting in poor academic performance and growth for students. A dynamic change must occur that releases the potential and possibility of a better future for our students.

TPQ

1) What is the significance and value of relationships and having common goals? What is the significance and value of having common goals in relationships?
2) How does the simplicity of the one-room school house differ from the large consolidated schools of today?
3) Think about all of the educational reform movements over the past sixty years. What commonalities does each movement have? What impact is evident from each of these movements? How will future legislation that encourages privatization of public schools affect the concept of public schooling as we now know it?

CHAPTER KEY IDEAS

1. There is a need for systemic change in the educational system.
2. Functionality of education remains in preparing students to interact in society.
3. The educational system is stuck in tradition for its compliance and complacency.

NOTES

1. Alan Blinder, "Atlanta Educators Convicted in School Cheating Scandal." *The New York Times* (2015). https://www.nytimes.com/2015/04/02/us/verdict-reached-in-atlanta-school-testing-trial.html

Diane Orson, "Teachers Involved in Waterbury Cheating Scandal Return to School." *CT Public NPR* (2011). http://www.wnpr.org/post/teachers-involved-waterbury-cheating-scandal-return-school

Grace Chen, "Some D.C. Public Schools Caught Cheating, But Problem Appears Limited." (2021). www.publicschoolreview.com/blog/Some D.C. Public Schools Caught Cheating, But Problem Appears Limited (publicschoolreview.com)

Greg Toppo, "Memo Warns of Rampant Cheating in D.C. Public Schools." *USA Today* (2013). https://www.usatoday.com/story/news/nation/2013/04/11/memo-washington-dc-schools-cheating/2074473/

Lois Beckett, "America's Most Outrageous Teacher Cheating Scandals." *ProPublica* (2013). https://www.propublica.org/article/americas-most-outrageous-teacher-cheating-scandals

Philadelphia Principal, "4 Teachers Charged in Test-Cheating Scandal." (2014). www.cbsnews.com/news/Philadelphia principal, 4 teachers charged in test-cheating scandal—CBS News

2. ASCD. "What is the Purpose of Education?" (2012). https//www.ascd.org/ASCD/pdf/journals/ed_update/eu201207_infographic.pdf

Part 1

THE SETTING

Chapter 2

A Story of Three School Districts
The Setting

Invoke emotion to establish change.
—Portia S. Bonner

What happens when "you" are the superintendent of a school district trying to lead change and are headed off at the path by numerous obstacles that are forbidding success? Many times obstacles that are unrelated to the goals of education are distractions that take time, money, and energy away from the goals, mission, and vision of the school district. This word "change" is used so easily in phrases such as:

We need change!
We are the lowest-performing school district! We need change!
We are at the bottom of the barrel, we need change!

Change tells us that we need to make something different! For example, change the curriculum, change instruction, change the assessment, change the standards, change expectations, change how staff are evaluated, change administration, change the superintendent, or change the members on the board of education.

As an educator for over twenty-five years, and serving as an administrator for over fourteen of those years, there is much to be said about the reform efforts of the United States' educational system and the continuous obstacles that are preventing closure of the achievement gap. This book is written to discuss those obstacles in the forms of nets, trenches, sinkholes, and cisterns all analogous or metaphorical structures to holding us in a position of stagnate interconnected systems rather than forward thinking, through transformational change that better serves our students in the twenty-first century.

There are three stories about three different school districts: one urban, one suburban, and the other a transitioning district from suburban to urban that serves as examples of the struggles districts have in addressing these obstacles in the forms of nets, trenches, sinkholes, and cisterns. Not addressing the problems these images portray contributes to the lack of change within the public education system. The story of each of these districts is told throughout the book.

The purpose of these stories is to make the reader think about occurrences in our schools and districts and questions to invoke discussion and thought about reform. They are actual accounts of real-life situations, some very hard to believe, to inspire thought-provoking conversations or to make you have an "Aha" moment regarding how to cope or survive as an agent of change. The target audience of readers is all those who dare to tread into the realm of leadership with a desire to make an impactful difference in the lives of students.

Perspective or eye-view of the text is written in the voice of an educator that is in the trenches, trying to reach the level ground or even better an apex of success away from obstacles that hold her back.

SECTION 1: DISTRICT 1—TRANSITIONING DISTRICT

School District 1 is described as a transitioning school district of a small suburban town that is surrounded by postsecondary institutions and home to one. It is labeled transitioning because of the steady changes in the ethnic, racial, and socioeconomic makeup of the town. This is reflective of the national trend of increasing diversity throughout the nation. The town's population is estimated at 61,000 people, of which 40 percent are people of color or multiracial. This is a 10 percent increase to the demographics ten years ago.

Educational attainment of the community is reflective of the postsecondary opportunities that surround the town as 46 percent of the population have baccalaureates or higher. Education is purported to be valued as a high priority of the community with a graduation rate of 88.4 percent, but the district's performance on the standardized test is below the state's average.

The district with an enrollment of 7,000 students comprises eight elementary schools, one middle school, one comprehensive high school, and an alternative program. The district's enrollment is declining annually. A notable percentage of students attend magnet school programs outside the district.

Governance of the school district is controlled by a nine-member board that is politically divided with a ratio of seats for each political party as dictated by the town charter. Board members are elected on alternate staggered years. A Regional Educational Service Center (RESC) is within the town, although it services a regional area of the state; it provides a significant amount of resources to the district.

The district saw gains in many academic areas over the years but lost ground with changes in leadership and student population.

SECTION 2: DISTRICT 2—THE SHORE

District 2 is known as an old seaport city that lost its industry like so many manufacturing cities and has reinvented itself with emphasis on green sustainable renewed energy initiatives. It is the home to many nonprofits. The city's population is just under 100,000, of which 78 percent are Caucasian with approximately 22 percent people of color. Ancestral background of the town is Portuguese including Cape Verdeans with a growing Hispanic population surpassing other ethnic groups.

There is a strong democratic body over the city; however, the elected school committee is split by party lines as dictated by the city charter. Unique to this nine-member committee is that the mayor sits as chair.

Unemployment and the number of people receiving assistance for healthcare are high. Of the total residents, educational attainment of a baccalaureate or higher is less than 6 percent, and 11.52 percent have completed high school. Performance on the standardized test is below the state average and the graduation rate is 66.1 percent while the dropout rate is 12 percent.

This district is composed of twenty-two elementary schools, three middle schools, one comprehensive high school, and alternative programs for a student population of 12,650. For a thirty-five-year period, leadership in the district came from within and limited itself to any outside partnerships with community and postsecondary organizations.

SECTION 3: DISTRICT 3—NORTHWEST

A small shoreline town known for its dynamic shape, similar to a "hot dog," has a population of approximately 29,000. The town is thirteen miles long, spreading schools throughout from north to south. Many of the people are descendants primarily of Italian origin. As for employment, the main employers of the town are the board of education and the town's governance, apart from some retail businesses. Governance of the town is strongly Republican.

The district has seven elementary schools, one middle school, one comprehensive high school, and alternative programs for a student population of 3,100. Residents' median age is forty-five to sixty-four, which is considered to be beyond childbearing years. Thus school enrollment is on the decline.

Educational attainment of residents is 42 percent have completed high school, while 21 percent have a bachelor's degree or higher. Primarily a blue-collar town with a poverty rate of 9.8 percent, there are pockets of residents who have successful family-owned businesses.

Students' academic performance on state test is below or near the state's average. The chronic absenteeism rate was high but has declined over the years. Governance of the district is run by a nonpartisan board of nine members. History of the board's political affiliation is usually tied to the mayor's party. All nine board seats are vacant and are elected every two years, which interrupts and affects the sustainability of the board's vision and goals.

Although three distinct districts in size, number of school buildings, and demographic makeup, they all share the common struggles of sustaining educational reform efforts, educating all the children that enter their classrooms, collaborative partnerships with community and families, and relationships between the board and superintendent. Stories from these three districts are weaved throughout the book providing evidence, candor, and support of the perspectives unfolded in the text by way of metaphors. In the final chapters, strategies and solutions that evolved within the districts as they sought to fight the obstacles are shared.

TPQ

1) Think about and write a descriptive narrative of the school district in which you are employed. Use this narrative to respond to the following question. What distinguishing factors described in your narrative may attribute to sustaining educational reform efforts?

CHAPTER KEY IDEA

Descriptive demographics of a school district help to narrate the story of what obstacles school districts may face.

Part 2

NETS

Chapter 3

Nets That Capture

And makest men as the fishes of the sea, as the creeping things, that have no ruler over them? They take up all of them with the angle, they catch them in their net, and gather them in their drag: therefore they rejoice and are glad. Therefore they sacrifice unto their net, and burn incense unto their drag; because by them their portion is fat, and their meat plenteous.

—*KJV* Habakkuk

SECTION 1: WHAT'S CAPTURED OUR CHILDREN?

When describing a situation in a way that can capture the essence of meaning and be used as a tool to explain or critically analyze a problem, it is appropriate to use an analogy and/or metaphor. A net is a simple tool that is a free-flowing mesh of material or rope that is intricately woven together to produce a porous cloth, sometimes with a handle to hold the net in place. The net's pores can vary in size depending on the woven pattern. Nets are used, for example, by fishermen to catch fish or by entomologists to capture butterflies.

In general, nets are used to capture prey and hold it until it can be released back into its environment or placed into a container for later use. The prey may not realize that it is trapped at first and rest on the netting, but then it may begin to resist and struggle, possibly becoming frantic and die. No matter how beautiful the prey may be in shape, color, size, speed, astuteness, or agility, these attributes are all captured. As we think of the unique qualities of our children and the diversity that makes up the classroom, only those who are wise, crafty, or cunning risk fitting through the pores or breaking the webbing of the net and escaping the fate of those who remain trapped.

How uniquely made is the net, for it allows air and light in, just enough not to suffocate or kill its prey. Failing school districts are the nets that have captured generations of students, trapping them in a repeated cycle of mediocrity and failure, and finally dragging them to a staggering statistical expected fate. Analyzing a random sample of national data from high-performing states for Grade 4 (see table 3.1), we can see the percentage of students who are at or above proficiency. These numbers show that half or more than half of fourth grade students in these states are not meeting the set goals.

Such distinction is found in the academic performance, dropout rate, graduation rate, attendance, and per-pupil contribution. Readers are advised to take time to review national trends of performance on NAEP, PISA, TIMMS, SAT, ACT, dropout rate, and graduation rate.[1]

Gaps are prevalent in graduation rates among subgroups. Table 3.2 shows the ranges of students of color compared to the whole school cohort and white peers. Overall, in 2017–2018, the national graduation rate for four years of secondary level was 85 percent.

The ramifications of our underperforming schools stifle the potential growth of our young people and disable the economic growth of our cities and towns. Students of color make up a larger percentage of high-poverty

Table 3.1 Percentage of Fourth Grade Students in Five Selected States Scoring Proficient on Their State Math and Reading Assessment

State	Math	Reading
Massachusetts	50	45
Virginia	48	38
New Jersey	48	42
Connecticut	45	40
Minnesota	53	38

Source: Data was retrieved from the Nationsreportcard.gov 2019 state performance report. The national performance average scale score in reading was 219 and 240 for math. Scale score is based (0-500).

Table 3.2 Five High-Performing States' Graduation Rates for 2017–2018 School Year

State	Graduation Rate (%)	White (%)	African American (%)	Hispanic (%)
Massachusetts	88	92	80	74
Virginia	88	92	84	74
New Jersey	91	95	84	85
Connecticut	88	93	81	79
Minnesota	83	88	67	67

Source: Data retrieved from the National Center for Education Statistics, www.nces.ed.gov

school districts, while low-poverty school districts consist mainly of white and Asian students.[2]

Nets corral the catch, but the holder of the net or the one to cast the net determines who remains in the net, who is to be separated and placed into other containers, or who is to be thrown away. The "who" are our children and the one holding or casting is the institutionalized system of education. When we use nets as vehicles to separate, contain, or discard, it can do harm. So the question is, "What forces do we blame as holding the net and dragging children to their fate?"

We must consider the institutional structure and the shackles of tradition, such as the length of the school day and calendar year; class makeup; the political arena of cronyism, nepotism, power, and control; the leader's effectiveness to lead; the teacher's expectations, beliefs, and stereotypes; unions and collective bargaining agreements; the parent and the breakdown of the family structure; the community's changing demographics; the curriculum; the media; and the students' concept of themselves. All these facets intertwine to create the intricacies of the woven pattern of the net.

SECTION 2: INSTITUTIONAL STRUCTURE AND TRADITION

A school building is composed of classrooms, a gymnasium, an auditorium (cafetorium), and rooms designated for special and administrative services and enrichment. The internal structure of the school building may be an open classroom or closed concept designed around a thematic approach or driven by the four core disciplines of language arts, math, science, and social studies. Students in many cases are grouped by their chronological age and in some cases by their ability. A schedule is in place dictating the number of minutes instruction is to occur in the core academic areas and the number of days and/or seat time that constructs the school year.

There are rules, policies, and procedures in place that confines students to structures with limited flexibility. A school year is dictated by states' governing body, by setting the minimum number of days that constitute a school year. Some states and/or districts have extended the school year or alternate schedules such as a year-long school year with the purpose of addressing continuity and for preventing the loss of learning or gaps in the learning process, ultimately improving retention.

With shrinking budgets, limited qualified staff, shortage of facility space, and a changing enrollment, some districts have devised virtual schools or blended learning environments to address their needs. In some states, our school schedules are so fixed in tradition that it leaves little flexibility of e-learning during days when schools may be closed, for example, during inclement weather or a pandemic. Using technology, learning can be continued with lessons and assignments being transmitted via the internet, counting this toward the mandated seat time.

Agrarian calendars continue to set the standard for how long a school year should be or the contact time with a teacher to determine if a student has met the standards and curricular requirements for the specific grade. Schools never completely transitioned out of the Agrarian and industrial periods, which both are now obsolete! Changes and flexibility in our schools and schedules are forced by the ever-changing need to address the exponentially expanding operating school budgets and shrinking available funds.

Forced changes can cause new, innovative, and creative means to educate our youngsters through alternatives to the average six hours per day, five days per week, thirty-six to forty weeks per year, and twelve years for a high-school diploma (not including kindergarten and preschool). Such innovation includes blended learning, virtual schooling, personalized instruction, internships and apprenticeships, and mastery-based learning. These are all methods of instruction that can be controlled by the students' own pace, ability, and readiness to learn.

As we move away from tradition, innovative districts now see the value of grouping students by ability rather than the traditional grouping of students by chronological age. Instruction is more individualized by establishing learning objectives that align with where the student is on the learning spectrum. New ways of thinking remove the net.

SECTION 3: LEADERSHIP AT THE HELM

Inability to lead a school or district does not necessarily come from a lack of vision, mission, and innovation on behalf of a single person. It may come from the obstacles of not being able to effectively transform the personal agendas of key stakeholders in their pursuit of power and control. Such agendas could destroy or deflect anything that has the potential to help the future of young people. These obstacles could manifest as antagonists, people who vehemently criticize any sort of change and will not collaborate but would rather fight than see any plan (good or bad) be implemented, especially if they cannot control it. Nets hold things captive!

A district's centralized leadership structure is made of the superintendent and his or her team at the central office level along with the board of education that serves as the governing body. Collaboration between the superintendent and the board of education and working together for common goals with expected desired outcomes should produce an impact.

It is difficult to fathom that this body would fail to strive for the singular most important goal of providing the best educational opportunities for the children in their community, by preparing them to be contributing members of society. Although a singular goal, there are multiple ways to achieve that goal. Personal agendas that disregard this notion of singular goal are deemed self-serving, selfish, and egotistical in their means to carry out actions that elevate an individual to a level of significance without regard or consideration for the children they are impacting.

Signs of effective leadership within a district can be evident through the culture and climate, collaborative spirit with a shared vision, fostering leadership within the ranks, intentional goals with a focus on instruction and learning, accountability in the areas of academics, fiscal management with a means to measure these areas, and true reality of the children's needs. Effective leaders within the school community have the power to change organizations. Such change agents are those who are courageous and see potential in their reality.

TEXTBOX 3.1

Testimonial: Initiating Change

Sometimes it is evident that change is needed. This can be an unpleasant experience for the leader initiating the change. The relevance and fear of change are important aspects that need careful consideration. Educators must realize that there is always a need for change because we are living in a society that is ever-changing. When initiating change, the leader must remember that the ultimate goal of change is to improve conditions for all students.

When a leader embarks on a journey of change, there are many variables that must be considered. Leaders must consider and establish a relationship with their subordinates and stakeholders because these are the people who will have the power to make the change a positive or negative experience. Any leader who believes they can proceed through the process of change without encountering resistance is setting an unrealistic expectation. Most importantly, leaders involved in change must gauge the readiness and ability of those impacted and must be able to provide professional development. Change cannot be done in a silo.

One must remember that some members who will be initiating the proposed change may be termed as "difficult" because of their resistance to something new. The disagreement can stem from the methodology that is utilized or their lack of interest in learning a new initiative. Time must be allotted for educators to digest and evaluate the new methodology. Providing time to reflect on the new initiative will sometimes deter resentment and division. It is the leader's responsibility to find diversified ways to engage staff to initiate the change through effective communication.

Effective communication will illustrate that everyone has a voice and is engaged in the process. Utilizing the strategic plan allows the leader to develop a paradigm for change that is aligned to the engagement of staff for the betterment of all students. Always keep the betterment of students as the main focus for positive outcomes.

Empowering the staff to assist in completing the task is also essential in having a positive outcome. Through this process, the leader is confronting the differences, valuing diversity, and empowering the staff to be skillful and confident. This technique provides the perfect opportunity for change to be developed and initiated. No one should be excluded from making suggestions or expressing their opinion. This means of engagement will also allow the leader to view different perspectives.

Any school leader involved in change must be flexible because dilemmas will always occur. Being astute in the variations associated with the process of change will improve the outcomes. A leader cannot focus on change alone. The leader must always give careful consideration to those who will implement the change and the impact the change will have on all stakeholders, most importantly students. There is no set technique to use; however, being able to identify the problems before they occur by engaging and being open to the staff and environment will make the task of change easier to handle.

Denise Clemons, Former Superintendent

Leaders who have the ability to empower others and the willingness to adapt to change can build a culture and climate that is focused and intentional. Such intentionality desires the best for the children and community they serve. Significant outcomes come from such drive while ineffective leaders are okay with the status quo and are most resistant to change.

TEXTBOX 3.2

Leaders who have the ability to empower others and the willingness to adapt to change can build a culture and climate that is focused and intentional.

Collaboration and a shared vision of success are pivotal for a district to be successful. It takes more than "one person" but a whole community rallying behind each other and working together with purpose and intent. How does the community define a "good education," and how are we going to invest together to assure ourselves that we are doing our best, giving our best for our children? What do we need to do to obtain our vision? How do we know when we have attained it?

Leadership cascades to the school building level as principals, assistant principals, and lead teachers. Classroom teachers set the stage for the culture and climate of their respective buildings, hopefully, an extension of their central office. Culture and climate are also shaped by the mandates legislatively given by the state and federal government in the form of regulations, curricular standards, and benchmarks. Leaders must be able to balance the tension of all these things and demonstrate a willingness to adapt to changing conditions and expectations from all levels of stakeholders, both internal and external.

Effective leadership at the district level idyllically would include an environment of trust and integrity and the commitment of employees to follow the leadership's direction and guidance. Those at the helm are learners too, as they grow and develop through participation in retreats, workshops, classes, reading literature, and researching educational trends. They need to stay current on the laws and changing needs of the children they are serving, be competent in their craft, and have the ability to "steer the ship" with vision, mission, and goals.

A leader must have a clear road map of how to attain the goals and measurable variables which yield evidence that goals are being met. Chapter 5 further discusses the roles of the superintendent and the importance of building strong relationships within the school district.

SECTION 4: TEACHERS' COLLECTIVE BARGAINING AND THE RULE TO WORK

Unions purposefully were organized to protect the rights of workers. Such organizations ensure benefits, maintain the workplace environment, and ensure the prevention of abuse by the employer. However, unions have been a major gatekeeper to the ushering in transformative initiatives of change that could prove to move a district forward. As we continue weaving the story of the three districts, included are the effects of how unions can be contributors to the obstacles that deliberately hold children in a net or a force that helps the district forge ahead to transformation and improvement.

> **TEXTBOX 3.3**
>
> Unions have been a major gatekeeper to transformation.

In some districts, there are union heads that wield power that could overshadow the superintendent and board members. Collective bargaining agreements produce contractual language that often governs areas such as professional development, time for and on instruction, teaching assignments, salaries, hiring practices, seniority and evaluations, and all factors that directly influence student learning. Relationships between superintendents and unions affect the culture and climate of a district, one of acrimony and balance of power.

District 1—The Breaking of Bread

When one shares a meal with another, there is fellowship, trust, contribution, and communication. Once a month, the union president and co-representative met with the superintendent and central office staff. Union members always brought stuffed breads, both veggie and pepperoni. It became a tradition to break bread together before discussing pressing issues, concerns, and areas of need. Unspoken rules—respect each other as professional colleagues and be goal-oriented on what is best for the students.

Conversations would ensue on instructional practices and the initiatives of the district as well as the emotional quotient of the staff. Such meetings proved to be productive in making changes in the district and prevented misdirection. Discussions were not only limited to the mundane contractual language and complaints but also about moving the district forward and the inclusion of initiatives that were working or the removal of those that were not.

It was a partnership that reviewed practices, teachers' concerns, professional development needs, and time management needs. As a result, student academic achievement increased and staff morale as measured by climate surveys improved.

District 2—Breaking the Leadership

In the first year serving in the school district as superintendent, the newcomer wanted to do something special for the teachers. She was told that the morale of the staff was low, feeling undervalued and uncertain of the future with the leadership change. Because of the summer break, the superintendent had not met any of the instructors, only the administrators. Working with the leadership team, they planned the professional development focus for the year and the itinerary for opening convocation.

It was suggested to include a continental breakfast prior to the start of the program with jazz music from the district's Jazz ensemble. Leaders sent out a welcome back letter including notification to all staff about the opening day and the focus of the school year. The hope was to change the climate to one that was welcoming and kickoff the school year with enthusiasm and on a high note—appreciating teachers, highlighting students' talent, and lifting morale.

And suddenly, a phone call comes twenty-four hours prior to the opening day from the union president to the superintendent. "You can't do that . . . , teachers start time is officially . . . the contract states . . . you must pay us for the additional 30-minutes." This was the superintendent's formal introduction to the union.

Burst that bubble! Trying to do something kind for the staff was a violation of their contract. Not realizing a bagel with cream cheese or a raspberry Danish pastry was an indiscretion, the superintendent should have negotiated. The superintendent had not yet met the union president because of the summer break, he hadn't been available. He sent a blistering email to staff informing them as to what time they should report. Sadly, on that day, those who came early to fellowship received retribution and scolding from their union peers! The superintendent's scolding came as it was time to begin the program.

The administration had to usher staff into the auditorium and sternly ask that they settle down. If you could picture a school hallway filled with middle school students passing to their classes on the day after Halloween with very little adult supervision! This should paint a vivid picture of the experience! (So you could imagine what classroom management was like in this school district). And, the superintendent's scolding continued when a board member said the request for the staff to settle down was abrasive, and they were being treated like children.

Apparently, there were different standards of professionalism and respect among administration, staff, and board members. Requesting people to settle down with a soft voice and a smile along with the assistance of building administrators ushering staff into the auditorium did not seem abrasive. There was a level of expectation, professionalism, and decorum that was expected from these adults. Thank-goodness what was experienced did not completely lower the superintendent's expectation of staff's instructional ability in the classroom. Students model the behavior they see.

On the other hand, if the superintendent told them to "shut up and get to their seats" then yes agree to the abrasiveness. There was a guest speaker on that day, and the superintendent felt mortified by the behavior of the staff. It was a sign of a battle ahead.

Forging ahead with the community, staff, students, and school board's help, a strategic plan was developed to fulfill the vision of improving the academic performance of students by preparing them for college and changing the climate of the district. The union fought and challenged every step of the way.

There was an opportunity to receive grant funds to improve the district's Advanced Placement program at the high school level. Part of the stipulation of the grant was to give teachers stipends for their participation in the program and for the additional work involved. The union refused to come on board because it was in essence giving a select set of teachers a raise. Money from this grant would have allowed for instructional supplies, student resources, and after-school programming to support student learning. Children and staff lost out.

The union president failed to understand the importance of instructional leadership because he placed importance on workers' rights at the cost of opportunities for them. He purposely created an adversarial relationship with the administration by pivoting board members against them and not respecting or trying to work with the superintendent and other district administrators.

Members of the union were divided: even a group of young inductees felt the union was not for them and refused to pay their dues. Within the contract, if teachers failed to join the union and release their dues payments, the district was obligated to pay those fees. Many of the members stated that the union leadership was selected so that he would no longer do harm to the children in his classroom. However, he had indirectly stagnated the growth and progress of the entire district. Adverse relations continued with the union president throughout the superintendent's tenure.

District 3—No Breaks Just Sustain

Status quo! Nothing is broken, so don't change it! District 3 was similar to District 2 in the mentality of work-to-rule, but the difference was a forged relationship that respected each other's position. This ameliorated many issues to the extent that it conciliated concerns. Yet with the traditional mentality of workers' rights coming before the needs of students, rights came at the expense of student learning.

A memorable conversation between leadership and union representative at the start of the school year follows: "So let's talk," said the leadership, "our academic performance has not improved, and as we implement the new evaluation plan, we are truly learning more about what is occurring in the classroom."

And the union's response, "Well we want to ensure that things are done to the letter of the law and there is consistency across the District! So teachers' schedules prior to the start of the school day and after school should be set aside for planning and preparing and not watching students. Students should be in the cafeteria or some centralized holding area. Administrators should be watching the students."

"Well administrators cannot watch 200+ students on their own and address teachers' and parents' needs simultaneously," said the leadership. "They need assistance. Each school has come up with a mutually agreed-upon system that is working based upon the climate and culture of their building. Do you not agree that we must consider safety of our students, greet our students and parents and set a climate that is welcoming rather than looking like a cattle ranch that wrangles in the flock to the hallway until staff comes to pick them up? Let's organize our chaos better."

One cannot assume that union leaders fail to have a working knowledge or understanding of transformational change and the importance of students' academic outcomes. Nor will we not underestimate the emotional sense of caring for students' needs. Somehow there must be a balance of meeting workers' needs and students' needs in which neither party suffers.

Contractual agreements sometimes hurt the very ones we want to help—our children. It also pushes away the new, non-tenured employee. This opinion is not a derogatory comment toward ageism, but years of service do not necessarily equate to effectiveness and expertise. If we were to agree that students are the priority and we are student-centered, how would seniority overstep placing a non-tenured, highly qualified, innovative teacher who has strong pedagogy and a proven record of student improved performance in a position?

In relationships, many times there is one party that compromises, the peacemaker, while the other benefits. We need a relationship in which benefits are mutual. There is a direct correlation between schools of excellence and workers' morale and working conditions. Our net entangles us and the constant tension and impact of unions have a bearing on the reformation of school.

It is to our chagrin when we place more value on a veteran teacher who is stuck in a routine that neither challenges students, lessons are stale, lack innovation or inclusion of technology, and students are unable to see the application of information. Contrasted with a teacher who challenges her students to reach heights never expected. When we have to choose between mediocre teachers to comply with agreements versus the well-being of a child, there is much to consider regarding what is wrong in our schools.

TPQ

1) What qualities do you perceive as effective to lead in today's public schools? Why?

2) How has the tradition of the public schools as an institution acted as a net to hold children's potential?
3) Unions protect workers and ensure fairness in the workplace. What is the relevance of unions in this day and age? How can they facilitate or stagnant reform?

CHAPTER KEY IDEAS

1. Institutional structure and tradition of the educational system corral, sort, separate, and discard.
2. Forced change drives innovation, removing some of the tradition.
3. An effective leader is one who has the ability to empower others and has the willingness to adapt to change.
4. Unions can be gatekeepers to reform efforts.

NOTES

1. National Assessment of Educational Progress National Center for Education Statistics //nces.ed.gov/nationsreportcard/

> PISA—Program for International Student Assessment. www.oecd.org/pisa
> SAT—www.collegeboard.org
> ACT—www.act.org

2. National Center for Education Statistics (NCES)—www.nces.ed.gov

Chapter 4

Nets That Hold

Abandon hope, all ye who enter here.

—Dante

SECTION 1: TEACHERS' EXPECTATION, BELIEFS, AND MINDSETS

In a dated work but still relevant focusing on the influence of secondary science teachers' pedagogical content knowledge, educational beliefs, and perceptions of the curriculum on implementation and science reform, though the focus was on science educators, it can be generally said about teachers' expectations, beliefs, and mindsets that:

> When educating students, teachers bring a plate full of attitudes, beliefs and strategies of teaching. Changing these attributes is more difficult than perceived. These attributes are the result of experiences they have had in the past. Teachers' beliefs, perceptions, and pedagogy do not spontaneously change. Such views are deeply rooted and tend to linger.
>
> The change process must be encouraged through positive reinforcement, support, time to try out new ideas and alternatives. Change is like an organism, it takes time to evolve. If we use the example of a highly developed species, change or adaptation to a changing environment is necessary to prevent extinction in nature. In other words, change is never immediate, but it happens through generations. In the realm of education, change is necessary to keep up with the times, the high demand for individuals with critical thinking skills and the ability to use technology. (Bonner 2001, 5)

Teachers are a necessary part of transforming a system to infuse new approaches, effect change, and drive change in the direction that shifts the current state of public education. "Teachers can be dynamic forces fully capable of effecting change" (Gabriel 2005, 2). Assisting in the change process, teacher leaders are considered to be co-agents of change, helping the district to move forward with new initiatives that require a new way of thinking and reflect on current practices.

Teachers' beliefs and expectations about their students' ability and the importance of what they're teaching hinge on the availability of resources and the conditions in which instruction is taking place. Critical factors that may impact teachers' perceptions on a child's ability include: stereotypes about race, language barriers, social-economic status, and the community in which the child resides.

These factors contribute to how a teacher formulates their mindset and perception of the child. Perception yields expectation of performance whether academically low or high. It affects the success of the student and results in the child fulfilling the prophecy of the teacher.

When expectations are low, the instruction is mediocre and fails to challenge the child's thinking and engage them in the learning process. The opposite is true with high expectations; instruction is engaging and rigorous with an expectation for students to apply and gain knowledge. Love for the discipline, that one teaches, impacts what is taught in the classroom.

Teachers who have an affinity toward the content area provide a better framework of instilling that same affection for the content matter in their students. But when instructional learning conditions are challenged by issues of classroom management, attendance, lack of resources, disinterested students, it confronts the teacher's ability or inability to engage and instruct students.

Below is a synopsis of how District 1 collaboratively worked together to infuse a model of change that resulted in the staff's culture shift of their expectation of students, beliefs, and mindsets.

District 1—Paradigm Shift on Student's Expectation and Teacher's Mindsets

District 1 invested time, money, strategies, and programs to improve the academic performance of all its students. The mission of the district was to "ensure that all of our students are reaching their highest potential," but as standardized test scores revealed a true yet disconcerting reality, they were failing to address the needs of all students. It was a district in need of improvement as African American students, socioeconomically disadvantaged students, and students with disabilities were not achieving the goal.

The district formed a partnership with National Urban Alliance (NUA), an organization that provides professional development for teachers to become more culturally responsive in their instruction. NUA's hope was to increase the partnering district's beliefs that:

> All students can be taught to use the higher order processes and engage in the advanced learning tasks demanded by a changing global community, and that race and poverty must not be used to erect insurmountable social barriers to academic success and life-long learning. (National Urban Alliance 1999; Jackson 2011)

NUA taught the district that it is not just cultural awareness but a generational awareness of how to captivate the audience in the classroom through the use of strategies that attracts students' senses and engages their minds to think by making connections in a way that relates to them.

In year one of the partnership, teachers were selected to participate in a cohort where they had conversations about the climate of their classrooms and the strategies they would use to engage students to become involved in learning. Such strategies included using thinking maps to organize thoughts prior to writing, problem-solving, or conceptually organizing information for understanding. Teachers were selected from four schools based upon their leadership qualities and the hope to share information with colleagues. The four schools included two elementary schools, the middle school, and a high school.

These four schools were identified as not making adequate yearly progress and/or in need of improvement. At the elementary schools, a consultant from NUA was assigned to work with the group of twenty teachers to teach, model, and coach the teachers with key literacy strategies to improve students' performance in reading and writing. During the first year, teachers worked with consultants approximately ten times including workshop time and classroom visitations for coaching and modeling. Many of the teachers participating in the first year shared some of the strategies with peers during faculty, department, or team meetings.

In year two of the partnership, the second cohort of teachers was introduced to training while the first cohort continued the second year of training. The journey to teacher buy-in and the dissemination of strategies had been a challenge, requiring courageous conversations about race, an understanding of the purpose for such an initiative, and the importance of teacher and administrator buy-in.

During the second year, the district also decided to utilize a trainer of trainer model to disseminate strategies throughout the district. An additional sixteen teachers dedicated themselves to undergo additional training to serve as teacher leaders for the upcoming school year. This group of teachers was relied upon to help expand this initiative throughout the district and encourage teachers to become more aware of the students' needs for engagement during instruction.

Employing such efforts was a fiscally sound way to ensure that the initiative would be sustained in the district without losing momentum. The district's heightened awareness of cultural differences capitalized on strategies that improved students' academic performances and increased engagement.

SECTION 2: STUDENTS' CULTURAL DIVERSITY AND GENERATIONAL DIFFERENCES

Students vary in ability, chronological needs, language, diversity, socioeconomic level, and the environment in which they live. Each child is uniquely different from the next and yet in most schools, we group children by chronological age with the expectation for them to learn a prescribed set of standards at each grade level. Grouping students by a single criterion attributes to the casting of a net over the masses, corralling children into the classroom without regard for their uniqueness or qualities.

We are educating a generation who has never known a world without computers and cellular devices. This generation readily has access to information 24/7 and sees no need for memorizing information that is readily available at their fingertips in nanoseconds. Their preference is electronics over toys. As generation X were growing up, Barbie dolls were the main thing for teens and now three-to-five-year-olds are the market for this toy.

Children's sophistication in toys has been accelerated with the demand for electronics at an earlier age. Instruction that has capitalized on technology includes web-based learning, virtual learning, blended instruction, project-based learning, and personalized learning. Even the inclusion of gaming through computer science is a means to introduce deep concepts of mathematics and science. These are all strategies to master the standards and learning.

In the midst of technological advances and the accelerated maturation of children, we still have challenges that hinder adequate education for all our children. These challenges include the belief systems of educators and community members and the child's capacity and ability to learn based upon indirect or direct influences of poverty, ethnicity, and race. These attributes are considered drawbacks to what a child is expected to learn.

Still, the norm is the phenomenon of white flight out of a community with an influx of diversity, or the ability to place one's child into a private setting with the hope of separating them for a better education. While families of color flock to the urban centers where jobs are available, housing and rent are reasonable, and other necessities of life are accessible.

Separating only fails to prepare the child for the reality of the world; it is vastly diverse. It is an inherent belief that given the right environment in which conditions are structured and nurturing, any child can grow! Such an environment must be welcoming, safe and provides conditions that are loving.

The word love is such a simple word but seems to be escaping our vocabulary, and actions of love involve more than just being tolerant but instead embracing the children, families, and community that one is serving. Love celebrates and recognizes differences, and these differences can be used to enhance learning.

Teaching is intentional, focused, and purposeful with an expected outcome in an allotted time: not just breezing through the curriculum to meet standards to prepare for test items but teaching our children how to "think," "construct," and "create." Teaching them how to decipher and discern; how to communicate their thoughts and ideas.

When caring for an unborn child during the gestation period, the unborn requires essentials that the baby will need to grow and develop. A baby needs food, shelter, clothing, protection, and love. Kept safe in the womb, a baby is provided with a nurturing environment. It is conducive and responsive to the mother's diet, actions, and emotions. It is sensitive to its surroundings, music, sound, and touch.

The same goes for a child who is growing and developing. A child grows best when the environment is healthy, safe, provisionary, and adaptive to the child's needs. It is safe to say that when conditions are not nurturing, it inhibits growth. Conditions become adverse, with no or low expectation that a child will survive. In some cases, the child barely survives even though acclimated to the condition.

In urban centers, class sizes tend to be large, sometimes to the degree that it prohibitively affects instruction. Urban centers contend with the availability of supplies and resources, subpar qualifications of the staff, overwhelmed management, parents feeling powerless, and the community's concerns of tax increases to fund a failing educational system. While in suburban and rural districts, we are seeing transition as these types of districts become more and more diverse.

When boards of education and school staff refuse to understand the changing needs of students and families moving into the community, it creates inequity and disrupts the quality of the education needed for all children within their district to be successful. Rural districts are isolated and alienated from opportunities while suburban districts provide more opportunities. However, technology is helping to close the gap.

Classroom environments are challenged with addressing the multiple differences and needs of students. Often, quality use of time on learning is lost to managing student behavior. If teachers are not strong in their classroom management, most of the time instruction will be lost to addressing behavioral issues. Routines and clear expectations that are set at the beginning of the school year set the tone for classroom decorum and school expectations. Schools cannot be valueless "free for all-spaces" without regard for others, but there should be clear expectations on how we treat each other and ourselves.

> **TEXTBOX 4.1**
>
> Schools cannot be valueless "free for all-spaces" without regard for others.

In some cases where children are not exposed to such decorum, it must be modeled time and time again. Realistically some of our children come to us from two-parent homes, where their parents have already begun to establish vocabulary, foundations in reading and mathematics, and modeling expected behavior. The same could be said for some children from single-parent homes.

However, some children come to us from homes that have parents missing in action. Children raising themselves are exposed to poor models of behavior not knowing what is appropriate or inappropriate. Regardless of the circumstances, we are still obligated to educate every child and that may also come with the social and emotional aspects as well.

SECTION 3: PARENTS' INVOLVEMENT, ENGAGEMENT, AND PRESENCE

Frustrated and disgusted, pleased and expectant, the many perspectives of families who rely on the public education system to teach their child how to read, write, and think in a safe and nurturing environment are broad. Parents often are reflective of their own school experience and expect their child will have a similar experience. Some parents distrust a system that is ever-changing. Change is cyclical only to repeat itself in ten or fewer years with no or limited results that are impactful for many of our children.

It would be hard to imagine differently that a parent would have low expectations for their child. It is perceivable that every parent would want the best for their child or even better than the best! Parents want their child to have opportunities that surpass their opportunities, a chance to be "better-off" both educationally and economically. They want their child to be successful in areas that would yield a better life; an abundant life that is prosperous.

Parents' expectations about schools are that they are safe and provide a welcoming environment for both their child and themselves. Schools are to teach children the basic foundations and meaningful concepts that are applicable to real life. This will improve their life and prepare them to be successful in both college and career. It is expected to challenge their child to think outside the box and to be competitive with their peers. They want equity and fairness for their child. Parents want an environment that is loving, caring, and nurturing.

Parents can be classified into multiple categories based on their behaviors. For instance, the entitled, sometimes come off as volatile bullies, simmering and ready to erupt. There are some parents who, for whatever past experiences, feel it is their duty to "hate" the system no matter how good or bad it actually is. Either through their former school experience that resonates a note of mediocrity or a recent experience of their treatment when communicating with school personnel, there is no forgiving of past transgressions and all must pay regardless of any help, assistance, or reaching out. Someone must pay the price for "their" anger.

Payment comes in the form of retribution, purposefully destroying a person's character, the school's reputation, and passing out misinformation. A sense of entitlement that there is something owed to them. These are the types to make a statement such as "I pay taxes!" imposing their individual right over corporate unity.

Disenfranchised parents are the voiceless who have been burned by the system so many times that anything they say or do is ignored. They become quiet and detached, unlike the helicopter parent who is afraid to let their child develop independently and hovers around the school building and classroom. It is a result of separation anxiety, not wanting to expose them to independence too soon.

Another category is the fearful parents. They do not intervene or isolate themselves because of the feeling of powerlessness or their unheard voice, for instance, families with illegal immigration status. Albeit, there is a deep respect for teachers and that it is the teachers' job to teach. In the case of immigrant families, they don't want noise. When the school system neglects to send a communication in multiple languages, we add to the isolation, creating an uninviting environment.

Then there is the PTA parent . . . , the good parent . . . , the MIA parent (present but totally missing in action), the grandparent, and no parent for the children who are raising themselves. All these types differ in their attributes but exhibit common threads of "how does the school welcome them, include them, and communicate with them." School Systems have been commissioned to increase parent's involvement and to engage parents better. Research is clear and definitive that when parents are engaged and involved, it directly affects the academic outcomes of their child.

District 2—A Fearful Parent's Trust

Miguel had been bullied for months. There was a little boy in his class who made fun of how he spoke broken English and would treat him meanly on the playground. Unfortunately, all these mean acts never took place in front of an adult. Miguel was afraid to tell his teacher, but he shared with his mother each time the boy was mean. Miguel's mother told him just to ignore or keep away from the boy.

Then one day Miguel came home with a bruised arm, and his mother asked what happened. Miguel responded that the little boy hit him for no reason today. Miguel's mother had enough. The superintendent was visiting the school for her monthly parent coffee clutch that week. Miguel's mother waited to speak to the superintendent after all the parents left the meeting. She pulled the superintendent aside and asked if she could speak with her outside. Before Miguel's mother began to share about her son, she quickly said, "I don't want to cause any trouble."

Miguel's family was illegal immigrants. She began to share her son's story and pleaded for help that would not divulge any information to the bully's family that may cause trouble for them. She feared retribution from the boy's family, community, and the school department. She did not trust the principal to be fair in her dealings with the situation.

A few years earlier, this community was subjected to a raid on illegal immigrants by the Immigration and Customs Enforcement (ICE). It affected the school department greatly because in many cases there were no adults to send the children home too. In reaction, the district retained students until a guardian, whether a neighbor or a close relative, could assure care. Now most districts have a family preparedness plan in place in response to the possible separation of a child from their guardian who may be detained or deported due to immigration enforcement.

District 3—Partnering with Families

Homeschooled for kindergarten and first grade, this now second grader had difficulty assimilating with his peers. His mother felt it was time for him to enter the public school system and socialize with other children.

At the time, the boy had a strong bond with his grandfather who he worshiped. He did not want to let him out of his sight. His grandfather was aging and also suffering from a debilitating disease. Some of the attachment to the grandfather was fear of losing him to death, as the grandmother had passed earlier that year. Separation anxiety truly affected the boy's assimilation into school life and his classroom.

It took weeks for the boy's mother, school social worker, principal, teacher, and cooperative grandfather to work with the boy. The grandfather was co-dependent too and put his grief of losing his wife on the boy. Over numerous weeks, the grandfather would actually go to school with the boy. Each week, the team would lessen the amount of time the grandfather was in school with the boy. Eventually, the boy was able to spend a full day in school independently.

Today's family structure is no longer simple to define, but there is still a need for partnership between family and school for children to be successful. Over the years, policies and laws have given schools more parental control over the children (loco parentis). If we estimate the amount of time teachers spend interacting with students over the course of a school day and year, we would see on average educators spend more time impacting the child than the parent.

Teachers have a great deal of influence over shaping the character and values of their students. Broken homes or dysfunctional home life affects the child to the degree of limiting a child's potential or academic growth. Students with less social-emotional drama of home life are at liberty to focus on their academic studies. Worry of basic needs is replaced with assurances that such needs are provided for, and their effort can be focused on learning.

Schools and family partnerships are beneficial in sharing the load of educating the whole child, better understanding of what their child should be learning, knowledge of policies and programs available, and networking with other families. Flipside to this, staff garner increased knowledge of the assets of the families and communities in which they work, appreciate the diversity, and culturally respond to such diversity via practices.

Partnerships improve the effectiveness of schools in attaining the common goals of learning and improvement. When families' relational trust is increased, they have confidence in the educational system, their local district, and the child's school. It changes the dynamics for all involved.

SECTION 4: COMMUNITY OF HAVE AND HAVE NOTS

There is an ever-growing acceleration of diverse communities throughout the nation. Both natural and social sciences help to define a community as a collective group of any size whose members are social, reside in a specific locality, have a governance structure, and often have a common cultural and historical heritage. Internally, a community may be more diverse in its cultural heritage and economic status. Historically, some communities strategically kept individuals out who may not meet shared beliefs, cultural backgrounds, or financial status.

Trespasses of the nation, segregation based upon ethnic group, religious belief, and socioeconomic status—although not as prolific and pervasive, these still subtly exist. Smith is no longer the most common surname but is replaced with Rodriquez. Fair housing laws that prevent steering and blockbusting of neighborhoods place limits on segregating although there is more density of racial diversity in urban centers than suburban and rural areas.

Socioeconomic pressures play a large role in where people reside. Of course, this directly affects which schools children attend. There are some exceptions to this, school districts that have magnet schools and/or charter schools provide more choices for families. However, the majority of parents feel very little control in deciding where their child attends school. Again the net rears its mesh with parents' limited choices for their child's schooling.

What value does a community place on educating its youngsters? What is the expected outcome of the investment? What does it promise? What are the needs of the community and how does instruction address those needs? These are all pivotal questions that, depending on how a community responds, help to drive the climate and culture of the school district.

TEXTBOX 4.2

The Community Superintendent

The importance and magnitude of community relationships are invaluable to the role of the superintendent. It serves as a vehicle by which external stakeholders will gauge your ability to leverage your social skills to engage others, observe your communication style when it comes to transparency and inclusiveness, deploy a microscopic lens regarding your decision-making as you stand in your truth, stretch your political savvies as you maintain your moral compass, and most importantly, whether or not you are truly committed to the children, the city, and mission of the work in its entirety.

In this role, you are not only the superintendent of schools, you are also the superintendent of (Anytown, USA), which translates to the superintendent being intentional and purposeful as it relates to being visible, present, and engaged in each and every aspect of the community.

One should never underestimate the importance of forging essential relationships with not only internal stakeholders, but with external stakeholders as well. Connecting with local businesses, as your students will seek out not only employment with these agencies, members of this entity will also serve as mentors, and recognize the entrepreneurial spirit of our students.

Institutions of higher education partnerships are essential when considering pathways/options available for students, advanced degrees for staff, and collaborative curricula design and development. Non profits are skillful in leveraging grants and unique opportunities for our students. Serve on community boards, of hospitals, colleges, and non profits, as your presence in these settings serve as confirmation that students/parents have a seat at the table.

Be prepared to accept each invitation, as your presence, not your visibility, serves as the metric of your engagement. Every interaction is important, every partner should feel valued, listened to, and respected.

Parents will be your biggest supporters when your moral compass reflects a laser-like lens upon elements that constitute only the absolute best for all children. They have the willful ability to galvanize and coalesce insurmountable movements on behalf of the best interest of children, and skillfully amplify their voice and choice.

Parents will see you in their child's school, as it is expected; however, they love to engage with you within the community at local external events, restaurants, markets, grass-roots fundraising, charitable galas, or simply walking within the neighborhood. This form of interaction invokes a powerful narrative and an opportunity to enhance relationships within informal environments that are less structured and void of time restrictions. Every interaction is important, every parent should feel valued, listened to, and respected.

Forecasting the future of the district extends well beyond the district strategic plan, as there is often an abundance of issues and/or concerns occurring within these community relationships which will enable you to sense the connective tissue binding individual agendas into one. The ability to forecast these events ultimately affords you "lead" time to develop and implement a solid plan of viable action steps. Every interaction is important, every person should feel valued, listened to, and respected.

In closing, a third-grade young lady was selected for "best attendance" and was rewarded with serving as "The Superintendent for a Day," along with an invitation to ride with me in an upcoming parade. During the first half of her Superintendent for a Day, I asked what she wanted to be when she grew up, and her response: "I wanted to be a teacher, but now I want

> to be a Superintendent." Every interaction is important, every child should feel valued, listened to, and respected.
>
> Aresta L Johnson, Ed.D.
> Former School Superintendent

Each community is unique in what it values and perceives as being a necessity: such as helping a child meet basic needs, a way out of poverty and to prosperous life, or instilling in a child how important it is to give back to the community. Businesses and industries in the town or city have needs to fulfill, such as replacing employees when they retire or developing a workforce that is fluent in technology, or whether there is an expectation for college or vocational schooling.

Strongholds of nets are influential in holding or interrupting the progress of a student's academic growth. A system's view of education shows traditionalism in practices, policies, and vices. These are stagnating reform efforts making it difficult to create and sustain change. Yet it also reveals the imperfect equilibrium of the system as a whole.

Practices and policies should be constantly adapting to the changing culture around them. In a sense, this is truly occurring. But, the educational system is used as an instrument to indoctrinate changes that become the norm in the larger culture. It is the relationship of the educational system to other systems (i.e., government, economic, sports, entertainment, etc.) that fosters an ever-ending cycle of complacency and subtleness. Schools indoctrinate. Schools are microcosms of society.

Relationships between each strata of the educational hierarchy must be one of trust and belief that each member of the partnership has, and it is the capacity to play their role, trust, and exude confidence that each party is working toward the same goal. Leadership can only be as effective as the relationships that are forged.

We can say the same for teachers when building partnerships with families and likewise their students. Confidently, teachers must believe that their students can achieve beyond the stigmas and stereotypes intentionally or unintentionally set upon them. Teachers must address their stereotypes and perceptions of their students and overcome them to provide the best learning environment possible for the child to excel.

Changing the needs of students requires educators to employ practices that address these needs. Such practices must entertain the assemblage of collaborative partnerships that build trusting relationships, mutually benefiting each party.

TPQ

1) How can communities support education beyond fiscal obligation?
2) Describe a true partnership between school and family. What are the necessary components that ensure a fruitful relationship?

CHAPTER KEY IDEAS

1. Teachers' beliefs and expectations about their students' ability are effected by their perceptions of such attributes as race, language fluency, social-economic status, and the community in which the child resides.
2. Teachers are pivotal to educational reform.
3. Classroom environments are challenged with addressing the multiple differences and needs of students.
4. Parents' expectations of schools are to provide safe and welcoming environments for learning and opportunities of learning that range from basic to challenging.
5. School and family partnerships that exhibit relational trust dynamically change the outcome for student growth and success.
6. The community's needs should affect the climate and culture of the school.

Part 3

TRENCHES

Chapter 5

The Trenches

Leadership and Reform Efforts

> Conflict and the desire for change are what bring us together. The energy of the relationship between conflict and change is also what tears us apart. It is through this dynamic tension that the need to confront conflict emerges.
>
> —Edgar Papke (2016, 31)

SECTION 1: IN THE TRENCHES

In the trenches! A trench is a long narrow ditch embanked with its own soil used for concealment and protection. Trenches are utilized during warfare to tactically hide from the enemy. Those in the trenches are strategically placed and are protected from the enemy's artillery. Children are strategically and protectively placed in schools for safety and preparedness. But children are not necessarily protected from the artillery of the enemy; the enemy is the perceived working institutionalized structure of the education system.

Trenches are also naturally observed in the depths of the ocean, along the ocean floor. These are depressions that are formed by subduction. A great deal of seismic activity can occur along these areas of depressions where plates push and fold beneath another. A third explanation of a trench is its use for drainage purposes.

In this text, trenches denote broken relationships occurring within a system that can result in division. For instance, teachers and administrators—one side of the trench—are working hard to provide a climate and culture of learning: preparing young people to be competitive participants in the twenty-first century as technology leads the way in social interaction. While on the opposing side of the trench, board of education, policy makers, and the community members create stringent policies and inculcate doctrines that are polarizing rather than helpful.

Students in the middle of the trench are no longer under protective shelter and covering. Instead, they are inherently socialized to the patterns of the larger society. We want our students to be able to think critically and analytically, problem-solve, make credible decisions, and use their creative talents to solve real-life issues. But, we are also indoctrinating our students to follow the "herd mentality."

Schools mirror the injustice and inequalities of mainstream society by sustaining economic class structure and racial division. As an institution, the education system circumspectly has prepared students to be productive citizens of a growing liberal left-wing society. To further paint a picture of this metaphor, imagine the institutionalized educational system as one side of the trench and reform efforts and innovation as the opposing side. Students still remain in the middle, which we will call "no man's land."

TEXTBOX 5.1

Schools mirror the injustices and inequalities of mainstream society by sustaining economic class structure and racial division.

Students are subjected to the idiosyncrasies of the majority's leading. Policies and reform efforts may specifically speak to the moment but negate looking at the long-term effects, impacts, and roles such policies will play in the future of our society. Schools are the vessels used to change the norms and values of society. While doing so, they maintain poverty, incarceration numbers, racism, hopelessness, fear, and denial of self-worth.

Whenever the United States has a major crisis, we as a nation cohesively meld together for a short period of unity. Unfortunately, this emotional unity is short lived and we quickly return to the daily status quo of division. In most organizational structures, when crisis and conflict occur, it becomes the impetus for change. "Never waste a crisis!"—the most quoted statement of 2020. Crisis and conflict can produce a window of opportunity for change and innovation. Such change could produce means for reconciliation among opposing sides of a trench.

Unfortunately, we keep missing the window of opportunity when it comes to the educational system. Means of reform have been pretentious and onerously placing more on schools to address the social woes of society.

How do we harness the short window of time when conflict unifies us into the desire to change and actually change? How do we direct energy from this tension to build trusting relationships with those who may be on opposing sides of the trench? This chapter first looks at the internal relationships in the hierarchy of the educational system and then addresses the larger systemic issue of policy versus reform.

Metaphorically, the following relationships can be described as opposing sides of trenches: the board of education versus the superintendent and central office, central office administration versus school staff, principal versus teacher, the community and parents versus the school system, and parents versus the board of education. Students are consistently placed in the middle of these designated entities and are subjected to the interplay and fallout of what these relationships produce.

When considering relationships, they can either be unidirectional or mutualistic in nature. Mutualism is the desired effect in relationships where each party benefits from association with the other, rather than the relationship being one-sided where one party benefits while the other feels oppressed, devalued, or invalidated for their contribution. Successful relationships are built on trust. Trust is "forged in daily social exchanges—trust grows over time through exchanges where the expectations held for others are validated in action" (Bryk and Schneider 2002, 135–137).

These social exchanges reveal a person's competency and ability to perform their duty. In that, respect for the person based upon their competency, ability, and performance grows. The following section discusses the essential relationships between key stakeholder groups that play a role in the success of a school system and the importance of trust in building a unifying bridge over the trench that results in true partnerships. This section will suggest ways to harness the energy of trusting relationships to strengthen school systems' effectiveness.

SECTION 2: THE BOARD OF EDUCATION AND THE SUPERINTENDENT

It is true that for any endeavor that desires effective results, when involving many people, someone must be in charge. Relationship between the board of education and the superintendent is one of authority and submission. The board being the head, the authority figure, should desire to seek the highest good of all those under its authority and not to be abusive, dictatorial, or domineering. In-kind the superintendent is to be submissive, joyful to do the work of the headship. A perfect partnership reflects total equality of persons, knowing each party's individual roles without competing for dominance and trust.

The board is one side of the trench while the superintendent is the other side. The desired relationship is for these stakeholders to work together for a common cause, rather than be opposing forces with students caught in the middle.

Superintendents will find themselves many times sacrificing self, that is, the ego, when yielding to authority. It is a difficult balancing act, and there are lessons one must learn in order to survive for any length of time in a district. The board of education and the superintendent consummate the marriage with a signed contract until conflict tears it apart.

Superintendents are at-will-employees and serve at the discretion of the board. Data shows that the life span of a superintendent in a district is on average two to three years for urban centers and much better for suburban and rural districts. However, the period is not long enough to truly build trusting relationships and cause measurable change.

Boards of education, the groom, are structured to govern the policies of the district and to establish a fiscally responsible budget that not only provides adequate education but equity in the quality of education throughout the district. Adequate education is well perceived and defined as providing opportunities for students to reach their highest potential and fiscally ensuring resources are available for these opportunities to occur. This differs from the proverbial equity issues that the needs of all children are met, which may require additional resources for the lowest-performing students.

Members of the board are either elected or appointed with minimal requirements. "It is the political body in which the public has placed its trust, believing that administrators and staff will educate children at the highest levels of achievement" (Pandiscio 2009, 11). Part of their role and responsibilities is to select a superintendent—the bride, the CEO of the school district—who will lead with vision and set goals.

In December of 2002, the American School Board Journal published a short article that asked a politically provocative question: "Do School Boards Matter?" The article purports that through the democratic process, school board officials are elected from one of two camps, supportive of schools or not. Their purpose is to set policy and govern the schools.

Individuals selected for these boards are not necessarily, or in most cases not, educational experts and may not have children in the school system. Their investment could be predicated on concern for the welfare of the students and their future and the school's effect on the community. A second rationale could be for their own private political agenda, such as using the board as a catapult to further their political career or to foster an environment of cronyism and nepotism, which usually results in low expectations, standards, and academic performance.

Many educators and community members see the board of education as the single or major factor in a district's pursuit of excellence for all students. However, let's think about how boards are elected. Who runs for boards?

Who votes for boards of education? The board of education is either elected by public majority vote or appointed by the governing body of the town, that is, the mayor or first selectman.

In many cases, the board is separate from the town government, where the mayor may be an ex-officio serving on the board only to provide a vote to end an impasse. For some municipalities, the mayor may actually sit on the board; this, on many occasions, can be viewed as a conflict of interest.

In many cities there is a selection process, either through a political caucus system or through a formal interviewing committee, to place someone on the ballot. The requirements to run for a local education position are at best minimal, for instance, a high school diploma or its equivalent. In many communities, there are such well-developed systems that those who would like to run may be blocked simply because their political agenda is not in alignment with the majority's agenda.

A power play such as this strongholds any transformation or innovation that could occur, manifesting a power struggle between the conformists who naturally meet the status quo and the reformists who urge change to the status quo. In most cases, these officials are elected, chosen by the community to lead. Elected officials in return give allegiance to their voters, always mindful of the next term elections.

Who is voting? Who is casting the vote to elect our officials that have been selected to ensure our public schools are providing adequate and equitable education? The share of US population that is school age is declining, while the rest is graying, leading to reduced political support for schools. Voter turnout in local elections historically has been poor. Those who do vote tend to be older, whiter, and more affluent[1] resulting in poorer outcomes for minorities such as uneven prioritization of public spending. Low turnout for voting reduces the chance for the electorate to resemble the demographics of the population.

Urban centers exhibit the continuous divide of who has a voice and uses it in the political arena through the vote. Even to this day after the civil rights laws passed, there are minority groups fighting to make their vote count. The right to cast a vote and to make an impact is still an unattainable goal for some.

It is incredulous that the inhibition to vote has resurfaced itself from the 1960s. Some have become complacent regarding the act to vote or the right has been taken away (null and void). So many individuals from minority groups are either turned away from the polls or have entered the criminal justice system where the right to vote is revoked. Disenchantment with the current system and allowance of the prevailing systemic racism have existed for years. Sustaining the status quo has only served as an impasse to reform and a much-needed transformation of public schools which could lead the way in the twenty-first century.

Relations between the board of education and the superintendent impact the overall functioning of the system and the achievement of students. An ongoing study of school boards called the Lighthouse Project[2] shows there is a direct correlation between a board's effectiveness and students' achievement. When boards are dysfunctional, students' achievement is low. Traits of a dysfunctional board are those boards riddled with conflict, decision-making guided by personal interest, poor communication, speaking ill will of the staff and the district, and failure to build a trusting relationship with each other and the superintendent.

TEXTBOX 5.2

Relations between the board of education and the superintendent impact the overall functioning of the system and the achievement of students.

A chasm occurs producing two polarizing sides of the trench and placing students in the middle. "When positive board-superintendent relationships are slipping, the whole district suffers and students and staff live with the negative consequences" (Kimball 2005, 6). Highly functioning boards act on behalf of all citizens, including future generations. Collaboratively, they set a mission, values, and goals, and effectually implement practices that intentionally meet the desired outcome.

Superintendents must constantly be on guard for a plant in the audience to bring up topics not on the agenda, and a chairperson who entertains such items. Sometimes debate between two board members takes over the meeting or taking time to brief members of topics on the agenda when they arrived at the meeting unprepared. Or the need to address board members who do not abide by the consensus vote and publicly continue to disagree or boards that avoid difficult conversations that require tough decisions.

Cold calling, blindsiding, railroading, and micromanaging are all threats that impact the relationship between board and the superintendent. When dealing with such dysfunction, there is no time to discuss academic goals, curriculum, achievement gaps, attendance, and students' needs.

In warfare, belligerent dysfunctional strategies are signs that an organization is on the verge of collapse. This is called attrition. One side attempts to win the war by wearing down its enemy to the point of collapse through continuous losses. This is quite a different mindset than that of the board and superintendent working together on the same side!

The following vignette demonstrates the misuse of power and the tattering of a relationship of trust between a board member and the superintendent.

Misuse of power and political position to push an agenda, even at the expense of the safety of others, is evident. It comes in the form of an email from one of the district's longtime vendor who provides contracted services. The email has been modified to remove any identifying parties.

Vignette: Ascribed Authority

To: Superintendent
From: Contract Vendor
I have forwarded the following email to you as I am very uncomfortable with the tone of the Board member. Please direct me here, I am concerned.

Begin forwarded message:
To: Contract Vendor
From: Board of Education Member

I have advocated for transparency from the beginning. Male is the perfect candidate for the position and deserves the opportunity. However, I think I have been misled to think he has the job and then doesn't get it. It is sad because I just received a phone call from the finance manager and he just met with the superintendent and spoke to her about the position and Male. He said before he could say anything, the superintendent said, "He is not a good fit!"

So the finance manager said that the superintendent's mind was made up. What did you say to the superintendent? It is not her business what criminal charges he may have. He is your employee, for your company.

The schools have a contract with you. All of this was set up with the principal and the school in which Male would be placed. Male had personally worked for the principal in her home and at the school. I have been on the Board for years and chair the key committees. I have always supported your company with contracts. I advocate for your company, it is my voice that kept your contract from not going out to bid again.

This vignette demonstrates how tensions could grow and breach relationships on multiple levels. The board member's actions are unethical. She forces her authority on a contracted vendor by emphasizing her role as the sole reason for continued partnership with the district. She used another employee who was trusted and valued to approach the superintendent rather than approaching the superintendent herself. The superintendent is placed in the middle of a decision and used as the scapegoat for the vendor. She was pressured to succumb to hiring a less qualified candidate for the district in order to appease the board member.

Also, the board member pitted a principal against the superintendent's decision, straining the future trust of this relationship. Maybe prudish in moral judgment, but the board member was romantically involved with the individual and failed to disclose a criminal record that would potentially place students and staff at risk. Making the decision was ultimately the contractor, who could have hired the individual and placed him in a position outside of the district. The district had the right to deny the placement of this individual.

A conundrum of sorts, the superintendent wants to remain ethical, practicing integrity and doing what is best for the district, yet wants to appease the board member. Ethically, the board member perceives what is morally right based upon her personal needs. As for the superintendent, the penalty of payment comes at the expense of a poor evaluation rating and "no" vote for contract renewal.

Broken trust is difficult to restore and heal in the arena of politics. Trying to do what is right and best is not necessarily held in high regard. District decisions seem to be pitted against maintaining your job versus doing what is best for the district. Unfortunately, such decisions appear to be on opposing sides of the trench, with the students losing out.

TEXTBOX 5.3

Broken trust is difficult to restore and heal in the arena of politics.

TPQ

1) How does one harness and redirect energy from crisis and conflict to effect change through building trusting relationships?
2) Mutualism is pivotal for effective relationships. How can failed mutualistic relationships result in oppressive and devalued emotions? What are the resulting behaviors of one who feels oppressed or devalued?

CHAPTER KEY IDEAS

1. Trusting relationships are pivotal to the overall functioning of a school district, so much so that it indirectly impacts students' achievement.
2. Schools mirror the injustice and inequalities of mainstream society by sustaining economic class structure and racial division.

NOTES

1. www.census.gov Census Bureau Current Population Study (CPS).
2. Connecticut Lighthouse Project (2000). Strengthening School Boards—Improving Student Achievement. CABE (Connecticut Association of Boards of Education) and multistate coalition. www.CABE.org. Adopted from IASB Lighthouse Study: School Boards and Student Achievement, Iowa School Board COMPASS: A guide for those who lead 5, no. 2 (Fall 2000) NESDEC and ERS.

Chapter 6

The Trenches
More Important Relationships

> Large-scale organizational improvement does not occur in a vacuum or sterile environment. It occurs in human systems, organizations, which already have beliefs, assumptions, expectations, norms, and values, both idiosyncratic to individual members of those organizations and shared.
>
> —Ron Lindahl

SECTION 1: CENTRAL OFFICE AND SCHOOL BUILDING STAFF

Teachers can no longer shut their doors to teach a personalized self-made curriculum but must implement the socially accepted and approved curriculum. They are held accountable for meeting standards and students' performance on normed tests—the evidence used to measure such accountability.

Creativity is limited in teaching and is replaced with scripted lessons, fixed curriculum guides, and expectations dictated by governing institutional bodies that, for the most part, have become out of touch with the needs of students. Central office staff, including the superintendent, expects the mission and vision of the district to be manifested by what goes on in school buildings and, more directly, individual classrooms.

Relationships built with central office staff, mainly between the superintendent and the principals and, in turn, the principal and teachers, also have to be based upon trust, respect, and a singular-minded vision of the district's mission. Working together collaboratively and agreeing on the mission and goals—acceptable practices to help the district attain its mission and goals and measures in place to see if you are progressing toward both mission and goals—are all important elements of success.

Building and codifying relationships come with hiring and recruiting a staff that meets the qualities that the district desires in their staff and developing that staff by professionally engaging them in discourse about supports necessary to attain the mission and goals. Human resources, talent pool, or human capital, however the workforce in an organization is identified, want to find and retain people with skills and attitudes needed to do the work. Schools hire qualified individuals with certification, skills, and knowledge. It is also a desire to hire staff that is representative of the student body being served.

This is a challenge for some districts, for adverse reasons such as a limited pool of candidates or the cultural practices of the district. After hiring, it is important for the administration and board of education to provide conditions that allow people to grow and develop but also to function in the capacity of their talent and gifting. Such conditions must produce a work environment that is conducive to student learning.

Recently educators have been eagerly more focused on the social and emotional learning of students. Staff members, too, have basic needs. Maslow (1954) categorized five basic needs for which everyone seeks fulfillment; this can be applied to the environment of schools as well. The five needs are:

1) Safety
2) Physiological
3) Belongingness
4) Valued (esteem)
5) Self-actualization

Staff want assurance that these needs will and are being met, such as a safe working environment that keeps staff members from danger, attack, and threat. Has the administration put safeguards in place to create such an environment? Are rules, regulations, policies, and practices in place to protect the sanctity of the classroom, school grounds, building, teacher, and student? Schools have become so compromised by inappropriate student-staff relationships, active shooter events, mental-physical abuse, scandal due to ethics and other impropriates that there is no longer assurance that schools are safe places to work.

Staff must have a healthy environment where both psychological and physiological needs are met, such as a classroom with appropriate air quality, climate control, and appropriate workspace with modifications when necessary. Belongingness and valued—like any organization, if one's talent, gifts, and abilities are not acknowledged, one could suffer from low esteem and feel as though they don't fit into the organization. This not only affects an individual's sense of validation but also staff morale.

> **TEXTBOX 6.1**
>
> Staff must have a healthy environment where both psychological and physiological needs are met.

All of this has a bearing on the climate and culture of the school, and the organization as a whole. Lastly, self-actualization provides opportunities for a person to grow and develop with the expectation of giving back to the organization to help it grow and develop. Organizations want to engage their human capital to fully utilize their talents to beneficial outcomes for students. When this occurs, staff find meaning and purpose, yielding results in the desired outcome of improving the educational experience for children.

Management has to foster an environment that meets these needs. When a worker is deprived of these needs, it results in negative behavior, attitudes, and low morale such as absenteeism, withdrawing psychologically, passive-aggressive behavior, apathy, or even climbing the hierarchy as an escape.

Many times decisions to downsize, outsource, or restructure affects the morale and commitment of staff. Such decisions are mainly necessary to control and reduce cost and operating budget. Treating employees as an investment in human capital by providing on-the-job training and education, opportunities for promotion and collaboration, as well as autonomy improves the motivation and skill level of the workforce. Below is a vignette on the importance of providing growth opportunities for classroom teachers and its effect on morale.

Vignette: Growing Leaders in District 1

Providing leadership opportunities contributes to a positive work environment. Teachers are more committed and invested in districts that provide leadership opportunities and promote from within the ranks. Part of the organizational structure can assist with providing opportunities for promotion at the school or building to district level.

In district 1, there were plenty of opportunities for advancement, as a result staff retention was high. Teachers realized an unlimited opportunity for growth. At the school level, instructional coaches and lead teachers were given opportunities to work with peers to strengthen pedagogy, instruction, and curriculum. The team approach to planning lessons, delivery, and assessments added rigor, continuity, and assurance to equitable instruction. Lead teachers and coaches who facilitated such planning emotionally felt the value of their worth and efforts. Administration and board members acknowledged and celebrated the fruit of their labors.

At the administrative level, opportunities to serve as assistant principal or department head were considered a stepping stone to principal or director positions. The same can be said about central office staffing, where assistant positions could lead to superintendence. Organizational structure in this transitioning district purposely upheld this structure through the years, but when budget cuts were necessary, some of the second-tier positions were eliminated.

The political dynamics also impact the sanctity of an organization. Goals and decisions, as a result of bargaining agreements, negotiation, and jockeying for power, are not necessarily in the best interest of students. Scarcity of resources creates conflict, animosity, and inequity. Differences in values, beliefs, interests, coalitions to specific groups or individuals, and perception of reality create a power struggle within an organization.

An effective leader has to navigate through the extreme depth of the trench. This comes with addressing the different dynamics of organizational structure and systems to move the organization in the direction of change.

SECTION 2: COMMUNITY, PARENT, AND SCHOOL DISTRICT

Common sense tells us that schools and communities working together ultimately benefit the families that live within the community. It is relational. Members of the community may feel disenfranchised and disconnected unless they have children in the school system. Most are concerned with how their taxes are being used to fund a school system that may be failing its community. It is a poor investment with very little dividends or return on the investment. Yet the investment should be priority, as it is investing in the future of the community as well as the present.

The amount of investment is representative of the type of product prepared and released into the competitive global market. The product is talented youth; the preparation is an education that challenges them to be thinkers, creators, innovators, decision makers, and analytical reasoners. We are preparing them to be effective, employable, and ready to navigate a globally, diverse, and interconnected world.

Bottom line—what is important to the community? Statistics must give a clear indication that the school system is meeting the needs of the community's children and that it is going to provide a high yield on the community's investment. Such statistics include standardized test scores, graduation rate, college preparedness, and vocational readiness.

There is some debate about the validity of standardized test scores being a true measure of students' readiness as well as the subjectivity to grading; however, these are the standards that are generally used to measure the effectiveness of a district. Standards of readiness are set on three levels: local, state, and national. The virtues of these standards are contingent on the value the community places on education.

Community building organizations, advocacy groups, neighborhood groups, faith-based groups, community development corporations, business nonprofits, and institutions of higher education all can impact the dire problems of an underperforming school system by working together to address local issues and thus changing the way public schools do business. Community building is:

> The continuous, self-renewing efforts by residents and professionals to engage in collective action, aimed at problem-solving and enrichment, that creates new or strengthened social networks, new capacities for group action and support, and new standards and expectations for life in the community. (Report from the Rockefeller Foundation cited in Education and Community Building 2001, 4)

Schools' reaction to the partnerships must place emphasis on personal and institutional relationships as a prerequisite to change. This occurs through relationship building, partnering with community groups, joining forces, and being intentional, deliberate in the cause to make schools better. Both parents and community members are an integral part of reform. School systems could build strong relationships with community partners by:

1) Credentialing and training in programs that support the school curriculum
2) Legitimizing what schools and community groups have to offer
3) Addressing misunderstandings and displaying a willingness to trust
4) Voicing the challenges at the school level and how they impact the community
5) Defining measures of accountability together
6) Sharing power and resources

In districts 1 and 3, there was a partnership with Experience Corp Literacy Volunteers, a program that received funding from AARP grants and local agencies on aging. This program was a joint venture that trained community volunteers to participate in literacy programs in the schools. Working together, volunteers were trained with best practices for elementary grades that were in alignment with current reading programs.

Similar partnerships with community health care providers worked in the schools to provide wellness, medical and behavioral resources through school-based health centers. Working together to meet the needs of students, understanding those needs, and problem-solving together are powerful recipes for success.

Although these are only a few examples of working with outside organizations, partnerships of this kind can impact demographic factors of attendance, mental health, drop out and graduation rate, and academic performance. Sharing resources, such as providing space for services and knowledge to address needs, both meet students' needs and affect the entire community.

SECTION 3: POLICY MAKERS VERSUS SYSTEMIC INSTITUTIONALIZATION

Struggles for control always result in losers and winners at the trench. In a perfect utopia, there would be a united front toward improving education for all children. Policy makers, such as politicians, special interest groups, foundations, and groups representing religious, racial, and ethnic populations, all play a role in shaping educational policy and reform. Each group lobbies for their political ideology and affiliates itself with like-minded groups. For instance, educators and their unions tend to align with the Democratic Party, formerly known as the working man's party.

TEXTBOX 6.2

Struggles for control always result in losers and winners at the trench.

Bureaucratic structure, or the systemic institutionalization of education, has been long regarded as the major cause of gaps in student achievement. Chubb and Moe (1990) suggest that the alternative to schools operating within bureaucratic controls is to allow them to operate freely. This ignited the charter school movement. The enforcement of goals, structures, and requirements imposed on schools limits the freedom, creativity, and professional expertise of the educator to operate within the system.

Likewise, students are subjected to the fixed quotas of achievement, residential zones, set standards, and grouping by demographic descriptors. The joy of teaching and learning is prescribed and standardized. Our practices still separate students by race and ethnic groups even though segregation has been ruled unconstitutional. This is evident in our academic grouping, residential zones for schools, discipline, special education identification, bilingual programs, and opportunities.

Curriculum content is dictated by the majority and popular culture. Political ideas are distributed through the curriculum in our schools, for instance, the continuation of the removal of God from our schools was replaced by socially acceptable practices that neutralize belief and values juxtaposed to the original foundation of our nation. As culture shifts, what was once perceived as socially unacceptable is now the norm. In the world of trenches, someone is always going to be offended.

In reform efforts, we have set standards but not adopted a national curriculum. We have increased the threshold of achievement, hoping this will improve instruction. All of this comes with working in the confines of the special interest groups, and as a result very little affect.

Education reform, despite its efforts, has not eliminated the gaps of achievement, poverty, unemployment, incarceration, discrimination, or any other social problems. Too many problems to solve all at once, educators want to focus on teaching and learning! Education reform is necessary, so it can reform society. Education reform inherently saves other systems such as government, economics, business, arts and entertainment, and family.

Complexities of these interlocking systems are very deep in the relationships between the systems and the weight, which each bears. This seems to be the yoke of the education system. It bears the weight of the other systems.

Disruption and removal of the education system would affect the functionality of the other systems. That is due to the constructs of these systems and their reliance on the education system to teach or indoctrinate the beliefs, principles, and moral imperatives of the other systems. For instance, schools teach the importance of being a law-abiding citizen. This effects how one will interact with the government and participate in the democratic process.

Extreme depth, pressure to perform, constancy, consistency, sustainability, and ability to adapt to surrounding conditions, the educational system has proven to be malleable thus far. But this malleability has begun to produce a network of tunnels or depressions near the seismic activity of heightened tensions of race relations, diversity, equity, and political friction.

Our new questions come with sustainability of the educational system. Can it survive the constant barrage of change, criticism, and systemic inequalities that it perpetuates? Is the current system inclusive to all or exclusive to some? How does this shape one's political ideology of the education system and the life of a superintendent? These are the things to consider as we leave the trenches for the sinkholes.

TPQ

1) How significant is the local, state, and federal vote in deciding the destiny of a school system? Why or why not?
2) What assurances can administrators establish to create a work environment that fulfills Maslow's five basic needs of safety, physiological, belongingness, value, and self-actualization? What are the effects on the workplace when these needs are not met?
3) Can the education system as an institution survive the constant barrage of change, criticisms, and systemic inequalities that it perpetuates? Is the current system inclusive to all or exclusive to some? How does this shape one's political ideology of the education system and the life of a superintendent?

CHAPTER KEY IDEAS

1. In order to build staff morale, it is important to provide opportunities for growth, promotion, and validation of their contributions to the school district.
2. Partnerships with outside organizations can help to impact change in underperforming school systems.
3. Political ideology and special interest groups are shifting the culture and in turn affecting the schooling of our children.
4. Disruption or change in the education system impacts other systems. The educational system is where we cultivate and indoctrinate the mores of the current prevailing culture.

Part 4

SINKHOLES

Chapter 7

Sinkholes

Sustaining Reform Efforts during Political Tension

Disappointment can do a couple of things. It can drop you into a giant sucking sinkhole of depression, a place you have to fight to climb out of. Or it can trigger an epic mania to overcome the odds and transform failure into success.

—Ellen Hopkins

SECTION 1: SINKHOLES

Straight out of a movie scene, imagine the earth collapsing right under your feet as a cascading white frothy powerful wave knocks you into a sea of chaos. Water is a very powerful destructive force and yet cleansing and purifying. When water comes into contact with rock, it can erode it forming sinkholes. The US geological survey describes sinkholes as cavities or depressions in the ground, especially in anhydrite gypsum, salt beds, or rocks that can naturally be dissolved by water. The depression that results is caused by some form of collapse of the surface layer.

As the rock dissolves, cavernous spaces develop underground until the spaces become too large causing the ground above to give way. For instance, Florida and Texas have rock type that is very susceptible to dissolution in water. Rock normally yields a firm foundation, trusted and assured. But when the natural phenomenon of water uses its force causing weathering and dissolution, the rock no longer has a firm foundation. Because there is no external surface drainage, when it rains, the water stays in the sinkhole and drains into the subsurface. The eventual collapse could be minor to catastrophic.

Sinkholes sometimes occur under landfills because of the insecurity of the ground and the heaviness of the disposed waste, covered by (fill) soil. When sinkholes form and open up, they expose things that were covered, hidden, or forgotten.

In our traditional approach to education, we have piled a great deal of fill, layers and layers with no reprieve in sight. These layers consist of legislative policies and politics, fiscal allocation of resources, pedagogical approach to curriculum, and the heaviness of assessments for accountability purposes.

Politics or the political affairs that are concerned with the production, allocation, and use of decision-making powers are viewed as a system itself. Their effect on the educational system is apparent in funding, policy, and control of "what" and "how" curriculum is taught. All of this is shaped by culture and mores.

Today's hyperpolarized political climate wants to categorize educational efforts as either right or wrong. Trying to remain neutral on hot issues—such as critical race theory, antimasking and Covid mitigation strategies, gender neutrality, "woke" culture, Black Lives Matter movement, equity and diversity, Proud Boys, socialism, and DACA, and the list can continue—by straddling the fence or being politically polite is also perceived as being politically charged.

Lately, school boards have been at war with the counterculture of the day. Contentious issues facing boards and parents voicing concerns, opinions, and their rights as parents are at crossroads. There have always been some contentious issues in education, for instance, the theory of evolution or removal of prayer in schools. Parents, who disagreed with the belief system, would simply choose an alternative means to educating their child. Conformity to the educational system's choices is an indicator of parents slowly relinquishing their rights to decide what values they want to teach their children.

Power struggles or competing for control in a particular sphere elicits responses or reactions from those who have opposing judgment, values, or stance. This creates tension and potentially division that breaks the trust of any relationship.

As the educational system shifts to becoming more and more liberal in curriculum, instruction, and enculturation, students are developing either a critical attitude or an accepting stance toward societal issues based upon their school district's influence. The education system is in a tense season.

Contributing to the collapse of the educational system from under our feet are the political and economic climates and reform efforts' inability to sustain systemic practices. Some of the factors to consider are the superintendent's lifespan in a district, the dysfunctionality of school boards, inadequate school funding, and the revolving door of pedagogical practices that affect curricular decisions.

SECTION 2: POLITICAL TIDE AND TURNOVER IN DISTRICT LEADERSHIP

Both the political tide and turnover rate of leadership in school districts are perfunctory of an eroding system of ethics, trust, and poor relationships. Emblematic of a sinkhole that is collecting standing water, never truly progressing toward improvement but wearing down a system until it collapses. Cavities or depressions and pockets of failure in our systems are intentionally designed to weather away the potentiality of success for some of our children. It can become a "giant sucking sinkhole of depression, a place you have to fight to climb out of."

A superintendent's lifespan is contingent upon the political will of the board. New elections in the crosshairs of negotiating a new contract can send a superintendent on edge or quickly looking for the next position. Relationship between the superintendent and the school board as discussed in chapter 3 is bound to the seated political party that is controlling and governing. This includes the mayor and his allegiance, members of the board of education, and staff who are politically and relationally connected.

TEXTBOX 7.1

There are risks to being a superintendent. No safety nets; contracts are limited; and boards change. Superintendents are at-will employees.

The school department in many cases becomes the employing agency of the municipality or town. Cronyism, nepotism, and political will are forces that greatly impact the effectiveness of a school district on the whole. Selection of staff is sometimes based upon the manipulation of factors to block those with ability, for those who can be easily micromanaged to do the bidding of the potential party in control.

Superintendents are sometimes selected based upon their malleability to submit to every desire of the political will as opposed to the ability to progressively move a district forward. A board member in a district labeled this powerful control and manipulation as "the Machine." She would speak out against the machine but in essence wanted to defeat this machine only to replace it with her own version of the "new powerful machine." Both favoritism and patronage seep into the crevices when it comes to hiring staff or creating positions to benefit friends and family members.

Some seasoned politicians (we cannot condemn them all) lose their way as they hold a public office. It appears that their concerns shift from a platform of purpose and principles to a stance of winning favor and retaining power. At times, politicians use their position to gain power or control only to exploit their position for their own personal gain.

District 2: A Case of Retribution and Retaliation

Retribution and retaliation were two powerful words that literally were strongholds in retaining the status quo in the district. Those empowered commanded an action with the expectation that the action would be carried out. If not, there was a strong penalty to be paid that not only affected you but the entire family. These penalties could be strategic character attacks via social media or the press. All contrived to meet the personal agenda of the aggressor. Too bad for the victim! A true cut-throat environment, where staff feared what would happen to them if they spoke out against the system.

On the other hand, those who had the political intellect and insight to work the system (or around the system) were able to survive with great impact whether for personal gain or for the benefits of their family and friends. Families and students are trapped in between unless politically connected. Many had no voice at the table. Sadly, a false sense of social justice and equity ensued on the surface, but if pursued deeper under the surface, the real truth to the matter would be revealed. Mediocrity would suffice as long as there was control.

How has the educational system sunken so low that the child is no longer the first consideration? Or seeing the educational system's importance as the means to securing the community's future in terms of economic growth? We have lost our way. Workings of a dysfunctional school board include issues such as the craftiness of an overt agenda for the public and the manifestation of a covert one when actually in the board room. Setting up pons to speak to their agenda or manipulating the conversation in the audience—all to distract the board from the main agenda, for example:

- Divisiveness of the board and members not conceding after a vote has been taken
- Argumentative just for argument's sake
- Speaking to administrators directly without the superintendent's knowledge
- Not reviewing agenda and resources prior to the meeting
- Micromanaging roles and responsibilities of the superintendent
- Hiring friends and family members
- Contracts to specific vendors for kickbacks
- Duration of meetings extended and drawn out
- Minimal focus on students' performance and achievement
- Destroying superintendent's character and reputation

Superintendents have to be resilient and acquiesce to the board's dysfunction when they refuse to change and work together. In the midst, continue to keep composure and respect even when the board does not display such civility; demonstrate flexibility and discern what battles to fight. It is really about the culture of the district, community, and board. Words of wisdom always see how long the last superintendent leads prior to their departure. Find out why the departure! Keep head above water, instead of trying to walk on water! Walking on water may be an indication that you cannot swim!

TEXTBOX 7.2

Superintendents must be:

Resilient
Flexible
Discerning
Composed
Respectful

Despite the dysfunctionality of the school board, for the most part, they are stable during service time. To our chagrin, that may not necessarily be such a good thing. If the school board member is truly invested in the welfare of all the children the system serves, then yes long-term commitment and service are preferred. Stability should lead to greater gains and achieved goals. Potentially, a school board made up of nine members with an election every two years could be a continuous rollover of ideologies, agendas, and beliefs that conflict with focused goals. Continuous change leaves a conundrum of goals but no attainment.

Same applies to the duration of superintendents. Reviewing the research in districts throughout the nation, the average tenure for superintendents is from five to six years.[1] A multiplicity of factors could cause the exodus of a superintendent. Most times it is in conflict with the political climate of the board. Changeover of political parties in office, vendettas, or retaliations could effectually change the face that leads the district.

Struggling to discern roles, the superintendent often clashes with board members, particularly chairmen of the board. Such role clashes are due to mistaken responsibilities. American Association of School Boards (AASB) has delineated clear roles for both boards of education and the superintendent so that there is no ambiguity. Unfortunately, many board members assume their roles without training. And because of long tenures for some members, the assumption is "we've always done it this way; business as usual."

As a new superintendent entering a district, press on spending quality time with each board member independently to get to know them, develop a personal level of communication, and then schedule retreat time so that relationships are forged. Sadly, some of the members may feel that retreats or setting aside time to meet are unnecessary. Especially after leadership has been there for over a year, the honeymoon period is officially over. Those who commit their time really are invested in making sure the relationship works and collaboration ensues for achieving the goals of the school district.

TEXTBOX 7.3 SUPERINTENDENT LEADERSHIP

The age-old question many ponder is whether leaders are cultivated or innately born with a propensity to lead. From the teacher lounge to board meetings, this question is at times openly discussed, and often debated fervently, especially when difficult issues arise requiring decision-making by a school leader. All aspiring leaders of districts should give this question time and attention. By doing so, they will gain clarity and understanding, thereby crystalizing a framework about their leadership.

Why is this important for aspiring superintendents, because how you view leadership will consciously or subconsciously be informed by your beliefs that ultimately manifest in your adult behavior. As the chief executive officer of an important public institution, the lens you use to develop and select your administrative team and teachers will determine your creditability and degree of success in moving a district forward.

The board/superintendent team will be profoundly influenced by your decision-making and how effective you communicate. Some decisions will immediately become consequential while others will shape the future by aligning to long-term strategic goals. Regardless, if it is a short-term issue or long-term issue, all your decisions will be critically scrutinized.

However, when decisions result in positive impacts on children and families, you will enjoy greater creditability. Creditability becomes the capital you acquire and choose wisely to expend to propel a district forward. It is the currency of school leaders and when understood, developed, and used judiciously, a superintendent is able to navigate an educational landscape that is replete with opportunities and obstacles.

The real leadership work commences shortly after you complete your educational training and professional licensure requirements. This is the common experience we share. However, school leaders vary greatly.

> Between your professional and personal journey, formal education, and your perspective on leadership, your tenure as a superintendent will be determined by how you lead a complex organization having many stakeholders. You will find yourself reflecting and refining your craft and understanding that some leaders may appear to be more natural than others but in reality, all effective leaders are evolving. What separates and distinguishes them apart are core attributes and their ability to discharge their duties with honor, integrity, and professional acumen.
>
> Hamlet Hernandez,
> Superintendent

A realization that some board members treat the superintendent as a foe, an enemy in the camp! A necessary evil that the legislative body states a district must have at the helm with a high-paid figure. Such thinking is unfair to those who truly see their position as a calling to progressively help not only the school district but the community as a whole.

"Good" schools lead to a better community that is forward thinking and invested in the future such that they provide an intellectually prepared workforce that is innovative and profitable and sustains the progress of the community's economic prowess.

Superintendents too must take responsibility for their actions! Many superintendents learn early in their central office role to respect the position of the board member, to be civil, choose battles, compromise without losing integrity, and watch self-pride. It is difficult treating others respectfully when the opposite sentiments are shown to you. But one becomes stronger in these attributes as challenges progressively come toward you like a head-on collision! It's as if you are a fighter who constantly gets knocked out, retreats to the corner of the ring regaining enough strength to come back out fighting.

Such challenges rarely ever become easier, but one gains endurance and is strengthened to take the stinging punches that keep coming. Your stride bounces and weaves and the blows do not seem as intense.

Vignette: A Night Out

Length of a board meeting is a telling tale that for many board members the meeting is a night out to be in the public eye. It is a period of time when board members can command attention from the audience and exert their power, with the expectation that attention is given and that an elevation of superiority is to be esteemed.

Even with an agenda in hand, the length of meetings are dictated by the banter of some and not so important discussions that center on such things as "Why my friend the vendor was not considered for the bid?" or "the meals in the cafeteria are not tasty" or berating individual staff members. Some public sessions become sounding boards for community members to berate staff, superintendent, and members of the board.

It is important that the chair stop such negative behavior by reminding speakers of public decorum, courtesy, and civility! And help the board to stay on agenda. One tactic is the board chair open each meeting with a statement of purpose and the board's role with the expectation of civil mindedness in decorum and public exchange.

When the foundation of the educational system is shaken by politics and economics, it shifts the stability of the whole system making it prone to sinkhole formation. Educational leaders must navigate around the areas of contention and hold steady to areas for the most part that are solid. What is amazing, very little in the realm of education is considered to be solid.

TPQ

1) What technical knowledge does a leader need to understand how to navigate the culture of a school district and its community? What adjustments may be necessary to adapt to the culture within the social roles of the superintendent and school board's relationship?

CHAPTER KEY IDEAS

1. Political, societal, and economic climate of the current day are contributing factors to school reform. Both policy and funding drive majority of the decisions that are made on the national, state, and local levels. Policy is contrived by societal or cultural norms.
2. Dysfunctional relationships caused by power struggles between the superintendent and school board or parents and school boards breed divisiveness and thus fail to envelop a shared vision. As a result, relationships are strained and roles and responsibilities are ambiguous.

NOTE

1. Superintendent and District Data https://www.aasa.org/content.aspx?id=740

Chapter 8

Economic Unpredictability and Funding

> If a man empties his purse into his head, no man can take it away from him. An investment in knowledge always pays the best interest.
> —Benjamin Franklin

Historically, school districts in the United States rely on local and state government controls for funding. Through legislative processes, the federal government provides assistance in the form of grants, both competitive and non-competitive, that supplement and not supplant state and local funding. Regardless of funding source, taxpayers are involved at all levels and are invested in funding education. We rightfully should be invested as the schools are preparing our future laborers.

On average, aggregate education spending in real dollars is trending upward. The amount spent on elementary and secondary education for all fifty states and the District of Columbia increased by 3.7 percent during the 2017 fiscal year; such increases are contingent on revenue. In the same fiscal year, 82 percent of local revenues for public school districts were derived from local property taxes according to the National Center for Education Statistics.

Connecticut and Rhode Island bring the highest percentage of local revenues. Property taxes fund the lion's share of school repairs, renovations, construction, and everyday functioning of schools. Property assessment and taxes vary from region to region creating real discrepancies in school funding within states, from state to state, and across the nation. This ignited the creation of equalization formulas to increase fairness in funding schools.

Public schools have become a burden to finance. Each state has its own school funding formulas using various criteria, variables to drive the ratio of determining how much a community will receive for funding the local schools. The methods and means of some of these formulas are so multifaceted and complex to the point that the average taxpayer must have a degree in nuclear physics to comprehend and compute.

Currently there are litigation, complaints, and concerns about the equity and adequacy of funding education. Connecticut is one of these states that is currently under fire for its Educational Cost Sharing Formula and how each community's percentage is computed.

Politics is a dynamic factor that can cause a cacophony of catastrophic events enough to cause a major sinkhole. As a matter of suggestion, a quick way to end the overwhelming economic burden of states and local municipalities to schools is to implode the system from within.

Increasing the cost of public schooling at all levels has become a burdensome task, with disparaging performance results. For instance, large and small urban districts are allocating millions of dollars only to be reciprocated with mediocre results. The cost of education should be in direct correlation with enrollment change, inflation, and the cost of living for school employees. Yet there are additional factors that warrant increases such as the changing needs of the students being served and aging buildings.

More and more, the public wants to see tangible and effective results of the money allocated to schools in the form of improved student academic performance, opportunities, choices, and services. Thus the evolution of accountability models linking increased school funding to improved performance.

For example, most of the federal funding is linked to ESSA (stemming from the 1965 Elementary and Secondary Education Act). Major grant programs under this act such as IDEA, school choice, charter and magnet schools, Title I and consolidated grants, and now Coronavirus Relief Fund (CRF) and Elementary and Secondary School Emergency Relief Fund (ESSER) in response to the pandemic are perfunctory of the political tide and the powers that drive the changes in the education department.

As of 2018, school districts are required by law to be more transparent with spending due to new reporting requirements attached to ESSA. This will further open the door for more scrutiny of equitability on how schools are funded on the local, state, and federal levels. Many stakeholders want to get at the root of district-level spending and student performance outcomes. Equity requires us to look at our policies and practices.

Most educational decisions pertaining to money happen outside the classroom. Policy and politics effect how education is funded. Laws and programs shape the funding at the federal and state level; this impacts what occurs at the local level. It is inherent that because of the historical local control of funding, there are large discrepancies in funding for public schools throughout the nation, for example, wealthy versus impoverished communities.

TEXTBOX 8.1

Most of our decisions pertaining to money happen outside the classroom. Policy and politics effect how education is funded.

Regardless, the educational system in its current state and means of funding realistically cannot be sustained. Multiple factors that include equity in pay, services, and benefits are exponentially increasing to numbers far exceeding what a municipality allocates for education.

Most recently our nation has seen more and more teacher strikes for increased pay and improved teacher-to-student ratios in the classroom. The rising cost of healthcare and prescription drugs are astronomical and affect both parties covering the cost. Increased threats to children and staff safety with the occurrences of school shootings have added additional lines to the budget for security staffing, equipment, and appropriate technology to provide some sense of safety.

Outdated spending mandates in some districts with curricular programs proven to be ineffective still remain and are an annual expense to the district. Insufficient and unpredictable cash flow during the fiscal year. For instance, while working in the State of Connecticut after the start of the school year, the state cut funding to schools. The first time in the state's history that educational funding was cut (this excludes not meeting the expected educational cost share).

Reducing your budget by 1 million dollars three months into the school year is no easy task. Such deep cuts impacted programs, staffing, and indirectly students. Special Education costs and the growing needs of our students could be the second largest percentage of the budget after personnel. Student enrollment is crucial to factors affecting the budget as well. Currently, in the State of Connecticut, we are witnessing a decline in the number of students enrolled in the suburbs and regional districts as families with school-aged children migrate to urban centers or out of state.

Enrollment affects the number of staffing, services, and facilities that are needed. Exponentially over time, one should see a decline in the dollars needed as enrollment changes, but this is not necessarily the case when other factors must be considered. Wise communities will strategically plan for such changes by consolidating their programs and assessing their facilities. The cost of operating and maintaining school buildings increases annually as well. Across the nation, many school buildings are aging. Some are considered environmentally unhealthy due to their age, location, and materials by which they were constructed.

Prophetically, we see the changing tides of schools no longer as the fixed physical buildings themselves but mobile anytime classrooms driven by technology that is becoming more available to us. Higher education is leading the way with more online courses and degree offerings.

We should not be shortsighted but start envisioning what this will look like for pre-K-12. Large school districts are already experimenting with online programs such as e-learning to accommodate the masses of students it is trying to educate. And most recently, the coronavirus and its effects on the economy have catapulted us into remote learning and rethinking pre-K-12 schools.

Torrents of concerns are being revealed as we see the disparities ever so widening the achievement gap, especially for urban students. Students who have access to technology, quality instruction, and a capable parenting figure at home have the advantage. Seven-hour school days will no longer be the norm or provide free babysitting for families. Questions do arise as to who will monitor the child while parents are at work. Of course with progress, new problems ensue. Uncertainty, volatility, and unpredictability of our economy and legislative body really caution how we plan for the future.

At the district level, it is important that there is transparency. Funds must be managed, allocated appropriately, accounted for, and connected to achievement. This is more of a challenge in urban districts that incur millions of dollars and aimlessly misuse the funds or fail to prioritize spending with the purpose of improving conditions for students.

Although speaking specifically of grant funds, the District Management Council in Spending Money Wisely (2014, 62) noted three key factors of why money (specifically grant funds) although this is applicable to funding in general are sometimes lost opportunities for student achievement. They are:

1) Scrutiny in ending ineffective programs and redeploying resources "to support higher priorities and more effective practices"
2) Decision-making on spending is based upon inaccurate information and then becomes institutionalized—"Well we've always done it this way!"
3) Compliance incentives (silo thinking) rather than district priorities.

As a team, the superintendent and board are to be good stewards of the money they manage. Having wisdom in allocation, prudent spending of resources, staff that are effective, strategic use of available resources, and working together produce a culture of excellence within a district.

It is important to take steps to identify each other's talents and gifts and acknowledge, celebrate, and tap into these gifts. Plan together strategically with clear objectives, measures, outcomes, and timeline, and, pace the team's work so that a sure foundation is built and progress is made. Build a strong foundation on financial principles and agreed-upon goals. Project or forecast the budget out more than a single year at a time and look long-term envisioning the future. These are essential principles to "good" management.

Interestingly, when it comes to school budgets, we develop and manage but rarely think of the concept of savings. Responsible managers pay bills on time and meet financial obligations, but there is rarely any discussion of investing for the future. Budgets allocated must be used in the allotted time based upon the given fiscal year. Rarely can districts carry over money into the new fiscal year, and the expectation is a return of unused funds. Rather than celebrating frugality, politicians will ask the question, "Why did you over budget?"

Vignette: Planning a Budget during a Recession

An annual event of a superintendent's life is planning for the upcoming school year's budget. One must consider student needs and enrollment, staffing and salaries, nonacademic operations, contractual obligations, curricular and extracurricular programming, and the health of the economy. All of these components weigh in for the consideration of improving students' academic performance.

It was time to develop the budget! A true blessing to any school superintendent is a competent, knowledgeable, and skilled finance director! In the first month on the job, the finance director educated the superintendent on the school funding formulas, the political arena of passing the budget in town, the coding on the software program, and the best reports to access for effectively monitoring spending. He worked alongside the superintendent with the goals and vision for the district in hand, a much-appreciated friendship as he and his wife became true trusted friends and allies.

Working with the finance director and the city's finance director, the district team was able to establish a realistic budgetary amount that was feasible for the funds which we were to receive and request from the town. All the department heads and principals submitted their budgetary requests aligned with their school or department goals to justify the request.

When it was time to reduce the dollar value of the budget, each department head and principal discussed what could be eliminated, what was priority, and what could be sacrificed. Very difficult conversations because to a building principal, everything is a priority in ensuring their school meets the needs of the children they are serving. The district was focusing on English Language Arts, literacy, and math; any request underpinning improvements in these areas was considered to be a priority.

With exponentially rising salaries and cost of benefits, the superintendent had to trim the budget by 1.5 million. In larger school districts, this is a much easier feat, but it is a herculean task in small size to midsize districts. Just entering a recession in the previous year, the rippling effects were felt. School systems are usually insulated from economic downturns or are slow to feel the impact. Creative budgeting absorbs the impact usually over a three- to five-year period.

During that short time, there was an increase in the number of students living in poverty, teachers postponing retirement, and improved teacher retention. Strategically, the superintendent did the usual hiring freezes, adjusted class sizes, viewed potential consolidation of school buildings and programs, and discussed furlough days. With much negotiation and consensus with staff, the budget was reduced.

As superintendent, there are multiple opportunities to learn valuable lessons. Even with foresight, focus, and intention, if you neglect the politics of the district, good intentions fail. While preparing the budget, the superintendent reached out to individual board members to discuss some of the reductions and cuts gauging receptivity of the suggested changes. The chairman was offended that the superintendent did not respect the chain of command. He preferred that the communication to respective board members go through him only.

Every district has its own culture and mores. Unlike districts 1 and 3 that fostered opened communication and discussion, district 2 fostered a despotic environment. Scolding is never a comfortable thing, but it is better in private. The chairman brought his notebook that contained notes from the superintendent's initial interview and started quoting some of the responses. Agreeable to his statements, there was nothing justifiable to his reaction, but his intention was to make the superintendent cower. A gently apologetically response ensued.

In the superintendent's former district, each board member had an independent voice until a vote was taken. This was not the case here. Acquiescing, the superintendent respectfully followed the directive of how to disseminate information. One must know the culture, if you don't, it counts against you!

Flash ahead into district 3, the superintendent was faced with reducing the budget by the same magical number of 1.5 million from the budget, but this time it was in the middle of the school year. This particular state had not been impacted like other states during the recession. While other states were coming out of recession, this state was significantly feeling the tightening of its budget, impacting municipal budgets. For the first time in this state's history, education funding was cut. This was a bigger challenge as the school year was already three months in session.

Again the faithful strategies were employed—hiring freezes, and so on—but this time the superintendent was able to introduce and negotiate a new health plan and renegotiate co-pay rates. With their willingness to negotiate, the teachers' union prevented layoffs and furlough days. Expenditures were reduced to meet the necessary reduction.

Transparency to the families and communities is critical. In district 2, the superintendent conducted neighborhood forums to share the overall budget and then more specifically how it impacted the schools in their area. Parents could compare and ensure that there was equity across the board and ask questions that pertained to their child's school. These meetings truly helped to build trust in the district and gave both community and family members an opportunity to ask questions.

Surviving cuts to school funding is a difficult task, as the expectations of that cost continue to inflate exponentially upward. Still recovering from 2007 to 2010 recession and now on the heels of another, school systems cannot keep pace with the needs of their students. States have a tendency to rely on spending cuts rather than a combination of cuts and revenues. Schools in like manner reduce budgets by cutting and redistributing their workforce.

Federal aid to states has declined in the way of Title I and IDEA; this effects what states allocate to local districts. The big business of running schools impacts local businesses and the community. Businesses want to shift tax burdens to someone else even though they want schools to serve their needs. People without children want to keep the costs of schooling down, and those with children want more money for schools without increased taxes.

Regardless of empathy or emotion toward taxes, the cost of education in this current model is increasing without yielding better results. How can we garner better services to our students by reducing recurring expenses? One way is to rethink the current model and discuss efficiency and equity of services for students.

TPQ

1) Serving as superintendent, how does one sustain reform efforts during times of economic unpredictability?
2) What does equity in education mean and how does a superintendent ensure that district resources are equitably distributed?

CHAPTER KEY IDEAS

1. School finance decisions happen outside the schoolhouse and are a result of policy and politics at the federal and state levels. This ultimately impacts the local control of funding within districts.
2. The cost of education for our children is growing exponentially to the degree that local communities, states, and the federal government will not be able to sustain.
3. There is some inequity in how schools are funded, causing both achievement and opportunity gaps.

Chapter 9

The Ever-Changing Pedagogical Approach

More important than the curriculum is the question of the methods of teaching and the spirit in which the teaching is given.

—Bertrand Russell

SECTION 1: PEDAGOGY, CURRICULUM, AND ASSESSMENT

Ever-changing pedagogical approaches to the content and curriculum are driven by beliefs of what is important based upon the trends of society, the political climate, and mandates of the groups positioning for control. Politics of the curriculum, content, and testing determine what subjects are taught, what is taught in those subjects, and what students should have learned.

In the 1950s, Sputnik drove the focus of math and science for our students so that we could be competitive in the race to space exploration and technology. The 1960s shifted the curriculum to focus on the disadvantaged students as the civil rights movement pushed for equality and equity in education resulting in the desegregation of schools.

During the 1970s society's attention shifted to career and vocational education and the accountability movement was birthed, and then a return focus on math and science in the 1980s and 1990s as the *Nation at Risk* report was released. At the turn of the century, the focus was on higher-order skills such as critical thinking and problem-solving, the so-called twenty-first-century skills. Districts decentralized the decision-making and empowered principals and school governing councils.

Last decade the focus shifted to college and career readiness, cosmetically changing requirements on the number of credits necessary for graduation.

Our current pandemic has shifted us to a virtual and remote distance learning platform.

America's homeland is experiencing a series of great shakings that are beyond the internal workings of quakes, eruptions, and shifting of seismic plates. Remember the metaphor of sinkholes formed by eroding rock and the surrounding higher land creating a cavernous depression. Let's start with the invisible enemy, Covid-19; it is stealthy, sly, sneaky, and random in selecting its prey. Economic fallout led to now-declared recession due to the protective mode of fighting the pandemic. And most recently is the all too familiar cry for social just across the nation over race, police brutality, racism, and equality.

Our children are in the greatest classroom of life right now, although grievous and adverse. Best lessons are learned in difficulty; it reminds us how precious the moments of life are and what to truly value. Are we learning the lessons?

From the spring to summer months of 2020, the curricular lessons across content areas included the appearance of a virus—Covid-19; its existence and appearance are debatable, but a science lab experiment has gone very wrong as it was released into the environment. We watched the manifestation of the virus go from endemic to pandemic in a matter of weeks. The math lesson involved word problems: how to stretch ten weeks of household bills with a $1,200 stimulus check and how to budget with loss of employment.

For social studies, remembering America's deep history of race relations and the skewed definition of race implies that there is more than one race—other than the human race. Therefore one race can be deemed superior to the other. This definition systemically and systematically infects every system that makes up the fabric of our lives. A fractional measure of a human being, three-fifths versus one whole, in our constitution designated some humans less than human. Unfortunately, this is part of systems thinking and still resounds in America's thinking.

Of course in our lessons, English Language Arts must be included—deciphering through the hidden agendas, opinions, equivocations, false facts, and social media post that leaves one's mind in a sea of abyss. Is it right or left? Is it blue or red? Is it democratic or republican? Is it wrong or right? Is it hot or cold? Does it matter or not? Take a stance and use the supporting literature to strengthen your argument, Common Core 101.

These lessons could not be replicated in a four-walled classroom. Educators could not conjure up assimilation this fantastic even if we tried. It is ordered chaos! Though these national events are shaping our new norm, how can we truly assess what children have learned during this hiatus and prepare to address the learning loss that has occurred since the shutdown of schools across the nation?

Learning from a distance versus face-to-face pedagogy has its nuances. School districts swiftly moved to distance learning with a digital component and some combined this with academic paper packets. Districts with an established one-to-one digital device model were advantageously poised to transition to a robust platform of continued learning while others struggled to purchase and disseminate devices, train staff remotely, and purchase software appropriate to their respective management systems to provide the basic structure and flexibility of online learning.

In three neighboring states on the East Coast, shutdown occurred in most districts in March of 2020. The states quickly scrambled to give guidance to districts. For instance in Connecticut, each district developed individual plans based upon the uniqueness of its community. However, most states received guidance from their state's department of education reducing learning accountability from achievement to engagement, using a grading system of pass or fail.

As districts gathered data of students' participation during this time, some districts acknowledged that 10–35 percent of students have not responded to distance learning. Of this percentage, some have no technology or access to Wi-Fi/internet. Seattle's school district reported on NPR that they could not account for the number of students who were not being reached further stating that logins do not account for actual engagement and participation. So back to the same issues, many districts contend with connecting to families that have long been disconnected from the system for various reasons.

Each school year, districts account for and expect some learning loss to occur over the summer months. This is known as the summer slide. Northwest Evaluation Association (NWEA), a nonprofit organization that develops assessments for districts, stated in a study that learning loss occurs and increases as students matriculate from grades 3 to 7. Urban districts especially try to combat learning loss with summer school and extended sessions. Can we imagine the learning loss that occurred and continues to occur in the nation's inner cities during this pandemic?

Methods of recovery for learning loss should look different in the year of Covid-19 and the years to follow. Some districts began the school year earlier than normal to recapture time. Others used the first few weeks to complete standards from previous grades and extended the school year with additional weeks. Smart districts had teachers loop with students where possible to continue student learning as they progressed to the next grade.

In the midst of all this, districts still have to contend with physical distancing measures. The big concern is addressing the learning gap of the vulnerable: the 10–35 percent who were nonresponsive or who had marginalized access to learning.

It is difficult to have neutrality in the curriculum; maybe it's impossible. In every core content area, you can find experts disagreeing about what is important and valuable to learn. Some groups will be offended, another disengaged, and another disconnected. Content may conflict with core values and beliefs, or it may omit essential elements of a group's contribution to the core, for example, history. This is possibly why our nation has never ventured to develop a national curriculum but only standards to help guide the development of a curriculum that is controlled at the state and district levels.

There is big business in curriculum development, textbooks, technical apps, and assessments. Each time new standards are developed or revised, it is time to renew resources to assist in teaching the new requirements.

In 2009, a meeting of governors and State Education Chiefs of forty-eight states, district of Columbia and two territories adopted the Common Core Curriculum. The goal of the Common Core Curriculum was to establish clear college and career readiness standards from kindergarten to grade 12 in English Language Arts and mathematics. These standards would be set across the nation and adopted by states voluntarily.

Pressure to adopt these standards were tied to race to the top funds under the Obama administration. Two interstate assessments—SBAC (Smarter Balance Assessment Consortium) and PARCC (Partnership for Assessment of Readiness for College and Careers)—were birthed to assess students' progress toward meeting the standards outlined in the Common Core Curriculum. The federal government pressured and interfered to drive education initiatives that were traditionally under the control of states and local boards of education.

During the Trump administration, the education department declared opposition to the Common Core and restored rights to states in determining standards. Regardless, Common Core is still pervasive and widespread throughout the states.

The attempt to address the problems in the educational system, through federal government intervening, only exacerbated the problems. Gaps in students' performance and equity still persist. A "one size fits all" solution ignores the diversity of our students and other variables of differences, such as the quality and style of teaching.

Reform strategies are stale, in that the cycle of new standards followed by new assessments is repetitive. "The basic failed model of educational improvement has remained unchanged: set arbitrary performance targets on standardized tests; apply them uniformly, without regard to circumstances; and reward and punish" (Koretz 2017, 173).

In 2015, the Next Generation Science Standards were released. Districts are scrambling to revise their science curriculum. The changes of these standards focused on the way in which we teach science by focusing on phenomena and using a storyline to prepare students to solve a real-life issue or a simulated real-life issue.

The pedagogical approach is very different from the traditional laboratory approach but seems to be a blending of discovery, constructivism, and inquiry. The amount of time for teachers to make this transition to the new standards is staggering, especially five years later we are still discussing the revision and changes.

Corporations who invested heavily in the development of science kits that each covered specific topics were popular at the beginning of the century. The districts that invested and even joined consortiums to offset the expense found themselves with an annual bill to replenish these kits with supplies year after year. It was an annual moneymaker for companies.

As most districts experience the numerous initiatives that a district focuses on, the amount of time, support, and the ability to sustain can be overwhelming to the teacher. Accountability systems and complying with No Child Left Behind, now ESSA requirements, have placed major demands upon the profession, pedagogical knowledge, and effectiveness of teaching in order to make significant gains in student academic performance, college and career readiness, and social-emotional learning. Many teachers are experiencing burn-out and dismay of the myriad of initiatives.

With the merry-go-round of initiatives (yes practices come back around with a new name but same practice), teachers have to see the benefits of such practices. So let's ask the following questions:

- Is there the belief and perception that there are benefits to investing in such a partnership or initiative?
- What is the value of engaging in these initiatives and implementing strategies during their instruction? Is it new?
- Is there reciprocity from central office administration and the board to support the work?

Responses to these questions determine whether an initiative is successful, effective, viable, and sustainable by teachers after training. It is crucial to have teacher buy-in at the start in sharing the benefits of such new initiatives or partnerships and expected outcomes.

Traditional professional development with one-shot exposure to a new initiative is not as effective as investing in a long-term training, coaching, and modeling framework that can span two or more years. For instance, district 1 used a consultant-teacher model for their culturally responsive initiative to improve school climate. Teachers were given the opportunity to learn, see the strategy modeled, and in turn apply it in their classroom as the consultant transforms into a coach.

Teachers were then able to debrief with consultants and peers to share their experiences and reflect on the benefits of utilizing the strategy. In turn, these teachers modeled lessons for their peers who were not a part of the original cohort of trained teachers.

Teachers serving as leaders have to lead the way for change to occur; they are the ones who have direct contact with our children. Teacher leaders who suggest the change and have conducted action research or pilots before going district-wide are helpful in garnering buy-in from other staff. Teacher leaders are capable of sharing information with peers and are continuously learning and engaging in professional development and modeling the behavior. Such teachers are able to put theory into practice and are trained in effective coaching.

TEXTBOX 9.1

Teachers serving as leaders have to lead the way for change to occur.

Not all teachers exhibit such characteristics. Lambert discusses reasons why teachers are reluctant to become teacher leaders. This includes "lack of time, misconceptions of equity, hierarchical cultures of authority, peer opposition, and a desire for harmony and safety over conflict and risk are just a few of the factors that discourage teachers from leading" (Lambert 2003, 39). However, we praise and appreciate those who are not afraid to take the risk for the advancement of our students.

Today's top five foci affecting instruction, curriculum, and learning include:

1) School safety, climate, and culture
2) Family relationships and partnerships
3) Blended learning
4) STEM/STEAM and coding
5) Personalized learning

Each area has numerous ways or strategies in how to approach or implement, but these are "hot topics" for the moment in the twenty-first-century classroom and overwhelmingly impact the direction of reform initiatives.

SECTION 2: SCHOOL SAFETY, CLIMATE, AND CULTURE

For years, educational researchers have debated the analytical separation of climate and culture as describing climate as the school's effects on students, including teaching practices, diversity, and relationships while culture refers to the interaction of the school's makeup (i.e., students and staff), and how these bodies work together and the set of beliefs and values that they share.

Climate is like the pulse of the school—is it friendly? do students feel accepted and a part? is it welcoming? is it like a community? While culture may describe the practices, beliefs, and values that occur within the environment that produces a healthy environment or not-so-healthy environment. Regardless, the terms have been used interchangeably to describe the environment of a school.

Although with the current and ever-increasing prevalence of school shootings and bullying, safety within the school culture and climate is still a hot topic and will continue to be, or so we thought. Now there is a political movement that is rethinking the policing of schools based upon recent and reoccurring events of police brutality. It is an issue that has turned in the opposite direction.

During the civil rights period, when schools were legislatively forced to integrate, there was much concern about the safety, climate, and cultural changes that would occur due to integration. Questions poised were: the consideration of the quality, qualification, and knowledge of educators in one school the same as another? Are additional supports given to ensure same if not similar opportunities are provided? Perception of equity and equality differs depending upon who is viewing and assessing it.

Are practices equitable or do we see discrepancies in how we regulate policies on students? There are higher standards in disciplinary actions for students of color and higher identification of males for special education—both are areas of concern. Such practices have become a direct pipeline to the prison system. Why such discrepancies? Is it because we do not have the tools, resources, or knowledge to address the social-emotional learning (SEL) needs of our students first before the cognitive? How can we create happy schools for our students so that they can feel safe and attend with purpose?

This taps into our beliefs: what do we believe about our students? Are they able, capable, and willing? And if so, how can educators provide an environment where they can soar? All are able and capable to some degree, but how do we deal with the unwillingness of which we helped to create?

Society and educators are partially to blame for this unwillingness. Generations of "sinkholes" that exacerbated stereotypes have stronghold students into underperforming. Parents' memories of their own negative experiences of schooling pass their beliefs to their children. Students entering classrooms expecting low expectations from their teacher find it easy not to disappoint.

> **TEXTBOX 9.2**
>
> Generations of "sinkholes" that exacerbated stereotypes have stronghold students into underperforming.

Beliefs and perspectives come from outward physical and visible realities that become ingrained over time. If this is all you see about a group of people, then it begins to limit your perspective, forming opinions, stereotypes, and beliefs that affect how one interacts. If a child continuously encounters a person who has a low opinion of them or does not value them, it affects their response to the environment they encounter. That response can be one of an overcomer, complacent, or maladjusted. Change the environment, and over time the child re-adjusts, thus the tremendous amount of focus on school climate and culture.

This is impactful for the classroom teacher because she has a great amount of control and management of what students will experience. Providing structure in the classroom with high expectations for each child and a classroom environment that imposes community-minded values changes the game for many students. Dynamics of the classroom become one of "respect and rapport."

SECTION 3: FAMILY RELATIONSHIPS AND PARTNERSHIPS

Part of shaping the culture and climate of a school and district is the strength of the family relationships and partnerships. Parents who are involved or engaged in their child's schooling impact the child's academic performance.

Involvement and engagement are two debatable terms of what is best and how deep a relationship the school has with the parents of their community. Involvement: such as assisting with projects, needs, and goals is important but is considered low-level partnering, while engagement includes or involves parents in the planning and decision-making, which is a deeper level of involvement.

School districts know the value of working with families. Without a doubt, systems that are effective, progressive, and high performing have partnerships with their families and have found a way to reach even those that are reluctant or untrusting of schools. The extra steps are to cross the barrier and meet parents in their homes, use technology, provide training to help them navigate the system, and work together to set goals for their child's growth and the school's progress.

Communication is so pivotal and as we become more enslaved to technology and social media, communication has become more immediate, visible, and time sensitive. As we build relationships with our families, ask what is important to them and allow them to have a voice at the decision table.

SECTION 4: TECHNOLOGY: BLENDED LEARNING, STEM, AND PERSONALIZED LEARNING

Technology has definitely impacted our classrooms and how we teach and learn. It is more than just a tool used for finding and seeking information but as a facilitator of learning. Blended learning uses technology along with the physical learning space working to complement one another by providing a personalized learning experience or can enhance a whole class learning experience. There are many types of blended learning processes such as flipped classroom, mastery, project-based learning, rotation/station learning, and self-directed to name a few.

TEXTBOX 9.3

Technology has impacted classrooms and how we teach. It is more than just a tool used for finding and seeking information but as a facilitator of learning.

Blended learning positively allows for increased opportunities in the classroom from online coursework to adaptive learning apps that can improve and teach skills. On the negative side, some feel that this replaces the teacher and limits students' interaction with face-to-face live bodies. We have learned during the pandemic that the majority of students still need that human contact that assures them that they are learning the skill.

We are teaching a tech-savvy generation that expects quick, visible, and entertaining lessons with bells and whistles. The screen has replaced the printed page. Even though teaching the same curriculum and content, we are now using different techniques, philosophies, and modalities with emphasis on trending career skills, for example, coding and gaming.

STEM, the collaboration of science, technology, engineering, and math are the perfect ingredients for project-based learning. Incorporating skills and principles from these disciplines to solve a problem employs cross-curricular work. The

STEM movement is plausible in efforts to increase students' interest in the fields of science and engineering and help to solve problems in our world. Math and technology are skill sets necessary to execute an actionable response.

So how do we incorporate this into the daily schedule of English Language Arts, reading, math, social studies, and science? Do we make it a separate class or can we do cross-curricular lesson planning? Will that destroy the number of minutes we have allotted for each subject of the day or can we count minutes twice to account for the time in each content area? And the poor elementary teacher who has to teach everything! When can they schedule this in their already busy week?

Our schedules and designed periods are so rigid that it limits flexibility in planning and delivery. Teachers feel the pressure of state testing and limit their focus to English Language Arts and mathematics. Very little dedicated time is given for science and social studies.

One solution to the enormous load on teachers and students is to personalize student learning based upon students' needs and interests. Personalized learning is a strong student-centered model that engages the student in meaningful learning opportunities. This approach considers students' level, interests, needs, and strengths, all directed by the pace at which the student achieves learning goals and demonstrates mastery (Zmuda, Curtis, and Ullman 2015).

TPQ

1) Part of a superintendent's leadership role entails curricular decisions. What is needed to maintain focus on the mission and vision of the school with competing societal trends?
2) What perspectives and beliefs do you currently hold about present societal issues that will drive your decision-making in curricular matters? How will you engage the staff, school board, parents, and the community in the conversation?

KEY CHAPTER IDEAS

1. Interference of the government and the economics of education exacerbate the obstacles of the educational system.
2. Reform efforts are cyclic in nature. Policymakers and educators implement a model of new standards followed by new assessments but have not addressed the prevailing issues of achievement and opportunity gaps.
3. Teachers are critical to reform efforts as they directly lead change in classrooms and share best practices with their peers.

Chapter 10

Accountability

It is not what we do, but also what we do not do, for which we are accountable.

—Moliere

Rigidity of the curriculum has affected teachers' morale. Schedules are designed with little flexibility in teaching content creatively. Project-based learning takes a great deal of planning, preparation, and execution to allow students to think, envision, plan, and create. The teacher facilitates, and it is not always predictable what the questions and outcomes will be. On the teacher's part, it is relinquishing control, and they must plan for multiple outcomes to a problem.

We become paper pushers with low-level expectations on Bloom's taxonomy or rotations with little objective and assessment of students' aptitude. Each child learns at his/her own pace, yet we group students according to age rather than ability and mastery with very little flexibility to change levels when encountering new tasks. However, teachers, when able, do flexible grouping.

Teachers are heavily burdened with teaching content skills for a test rather than teaching for the joy of teaching and learning. We are drill sergeants who no longer enjoy the craft and purpose of teaching. This is the sacrifice in order to score well on a one-shot assessment that does not capture the true knowledge of what a student knows. Teachers are stressed out, and students are stressed out as well!

Accountability measures are enough to cause the ground to shift underneath! Someone must take the blame for failing schools and it is not just students, it is not just teachers, it is not just superintendents, it is not just boards of education, but the whole system itself is designed for implosion. Schools are the only institutionalized system that has a "bloated agenda." Jamie Vollmere (2010, 111) in *Schools Cannot Do It Alone* stated that:

> Ever-expanding expectations: Americans now expect their schools to teach the basics, create responsible citizens, prepare effective workers, and respond to all the physical, emotional, and psychological needs of children living in a post-industrial society. It may be a laudable goal, but the bloated agenda disturbs many in the community. They intuitively understand that no institution can successfully be all things to all people. Seeing our schools make the attempt prompts them to reassess their commitment.

The pressure is on to raise test scores that are used as a demarcation for success. Tests are influential in that they shape what is taught and how it is taught (Koretz 2017). Test-based accountability is used to measure students' performance on a set of standards; in turn, these measurements create a competitive environment to push for higher performance. The belief is that higher performance on these tests yields better schools, but it is a deception. Testing creates an illusion that it is the answer to improving the success of schools and students and equity. But testing has exacerbated the achievement gap.

Testing has been a mechanism in place for measuring the success of students and schools long before *A Nation at Risk* (1983), *NCLB* (2002), and now *ESSA* (2015–present day). Using test as the only criterion to measure students' success limits the measure to strict standards. ESSA has expanded the criterion in which districts and states can build their accountability model to consider other areas in which students are succeeding.

ESSA introduced the accountability model where states have the authority to use other criteria to assess students' progress. However, test performance is still weighted heavier than these other options (such as attendance/discipline, CTE, participation in the arts, completing ninth grade courses, graduation rate, etc.).

Politics and the federal government are the sources of the testing culture. The original function of test was for diagnostic purposes to determine students' strengths and weaknesses. Now we use it to evaluate teachers, schools, and entire districts. Districts are rewarded or punished based upon students' performance on these tests. Sanctions of labels, intervention from the state, financing have become the result of testing.

Accountability models have shifted from holding students accountable for their own performance to a mechanism to evaluate the effectiveness of teachers. Students are labeled and categorized into the following four groups: below basic, basic, proficient, and advanced. The model pushes for students, regardless of disability and language barrier, to be 100 percent proficient on these tests. Mandated reporting of demographic subgroups: Socioeconomic status, Special needs, English Learners, racial/ethnic, migrants, served to create a disadvantage. Such reporting was an attempt to address the inequities in education by using single performance standards. However it widen the gaps.

The net effects of reform, the good and the bad, and the fragile foundation is a broken system. Accountability was the original purpose of assessment. It was a move to address the achievement gap, but the teachers and administrators who are pressured to perform created a culture of cheating. The inflation of scores rather than improving the learning for students became a practicing culture.

In order to improve test scores, some teachers teach only to prepare for the test, others teach test-taking strategies, and low-performing students and lowered standards are excluded. The administration targets only specific groups of students to improve and ignores the rest. Other strategies are to changing responses on test, giving test answers in advance, and giving answers during the test. (See www.huffpost.com/entry/educators-tamper-students-tests_n_895179). Teachers were also given pay incentives to raise scores—encouraging a culture of unethical practice.

Districts will reallocate funds to address the areas that are being tested and minimize the importance of the arts, social studies, and world languages. The whole curriculum seems to revolve around what is being tested.

The motive of why we do things is that the tests are costly to produce and are administered annually. It narrows what is taught, as most teachers target to teach only what is on the test. Students and educators are stressed out over the amount of pressure to perform. School schedules and life revolve around tests. There is very little room for educators' creativity, and most lessons are driven by what is tested. Educators all over seem to be given the same incentive—raise the scores and close the achievement gap. Affluent districts, likewise, maintain the high scores.

There is inequity in assessments, setting arbitrary targets on the test and the time in which all students are to reach such targets. The practicality of all students being on the same developmental clock to master standards at the same time is not practical.

Our education system revolves around performance standards. It is the percentage of students meeting the standards that determine the effectiveness of the teaching, and the school. In urban centers and poor rural and suburban districts, disadvantaged students clustered at the same school are trapped in a cycle of low performance. Deceptively, imposing higher standards on low-performing schools encourages a continued cycle of low performance.

Political and economic factors continue to erode the educational system and have thwarted reform efforts. Overwhelmingly, demands placed upon schools in regard to addressing societal ills and trends disrupt the original focus and mission of schools. Schools have become a perfunctory hub of compliance to the trending norms of society that are not always necessary for the greater good.

The educational system flows with the wind and latches onto the sails that set the trends. Educators become the indoctrinators of societal norms. This is evident by the recycling and changes in curricula. Although the system swiftly reacts to societal changes through its curricula, very little change affects the instructional approach, traditional structure of the school day, setting, and calendar. These artifacts of tradition remain fixed, serving as the base of the sinkhole, carved in stone as a testament to the agrarian society. While the ever-flowing winds of change are eroding the system from within, it is just a matter of time before it collapses.

Organisms living underground within a sinkhole amazingly adapt to its surroundings. This is equivalent to how districts survive in such a disruptive environment. Sensitivity to its surroundings, districts adapt by changing curriculum, pedagogical practices, lacking to address students' basic needs, succumb to societal and political pressures, and deal with the accountability at best.

TPQ

1. Accountability, the good, the bad, and the mediocre. Design an accountability plan that addresses students' performance in reading and mathematics. What diagnostic tools would you use, give a rationale. And to what frequency? As an instructional leader, how will you help teachers and principals translate data into appropriate instruction to meet student goals?

CHAPTER KEY IDEA

Present-day testing culture and accountability models have placed great demands on schools to perform. This has resulted in an erosion of what and how teachers teach and ethical practices.

Part 5

CISTERNS

Chapter 11

Cisterns

Empty Wells That Are Not Being Replenished!

Drink water from your own cistern and fresh water from your own well.
—Proverbs 5:15

SECTION 1: CISTERNS

Schools like cisterns have become storehouses, but of talent and intellect rather than rainwater. In many instances, educators are forced to teach to the middle or lower levels as accountability models dictate, often with small amounts of focus on high achievers or gifted students. Schools are receptacles that hold back students from reaching their potential, in some cases from aspiring above or beyond their potential. They are relics wearing away such as old dilapidated school buildings found along the roadsides of crumbling neighborhoods. And when empty, this signals evidence of drought.

Traveling abroad in Europe and the Middle East, frequently you would see ancient stone structures called cisterns. A cistern is a vessel that stores water; it is in some cases a natural underground reservoir where rainwater collects. It is a receptacle that a town would use to collect rainwater if there was a scarcity of springs or water systems. A cistern usually has a round opening at the top. During the Middle Ages in Europe, cisterns were constructed replacing wells that could not be dug deeply. In Rome, each neighborhood or quarter had a central cistern. Empty cisterns were sometimes used as prisons.

Description of cisterns metaphorically relates to characterizing schools as receptacles. Many of these receptacles are aging structures that keep students from achieving their potential and poorly prepare students for the future workforce and globalization.

Cisterns provided a needed source of water to its neighborhoods or quarters. The natural collection of rainwater was a wise way of amassing a needed, naturally occurring resource when available. But during times of drought, the cistern cannot maintain its rich provision of water. Very little water is collected during drought. This not only affects the availability of drinking water but the ability of farmers to water crops and to maintain the food supply. Droughts are damaging and could lead to relocating or dying out of whole neighborhoods or quarters.

Schools like cisterns mock the emblematic use of cisterns. To apply the effects of drought to schools, we can ask the following question, "How do we equitably distribute resources when resources are scarce?" In response to scarcity, we begin to open ourselves up to mediocrity such as in the selection and hiring of staff; lack of innovation and flexibility in the school schedules, programs, and instruction; and limiting opportunities that we are providing for our young people.

Lack produces a scarcity mentality; we limit our response to improvement based upon the availability of resources, such as staffing to keep class size small, technology, teacher training, support staff, and community outreach. Response to improvement becomes provisional by maintaining the status quo with the hope of some great windfall that transforms the district. And when the cistern is barren, it almost becomes a prison to hold students back from reaching their potential or actually feeding the prison pipeline by discarding those who we see as having no value.

Schools in fiscally stretched districts, especially the large urban districts, receive millions of dollars to fund education, but when the funds are misappropriated or spending is above the district's resources, even basic necessities become a challenge to provide. We find teachers purchasing basic supplies such as pencils, paper, staplers, and staples, just so that the learning can continue in the classroom.

Likewise, some small school districts consisting of one school building struggle to maintain quality of education with limited funds and resources. In most cases, they sacrifice quality and substance to keep the cost down.

Such inequity of resources and inadequate preparation of our youngsters affect the future workforce and the very foundation of our society's soul. Failing to prepare our students to lead productive and purposeful lives will lend to the demise and undergirding of our nation as it crumbles before our eyes.

SECTION 2: TEACHING TO THE MIDDLE AND LOWER LEVELS

Heightened concerns of learning loss and recovery, equity, and falling behind are at the forefront of educators thinking as we combat a national pandemic.

This pandemic has closed down schools and forced the expansion of virtual and distance learning. Resources are being redirected to enforce smaller classrooms and a duality platform to include both face-to-face and remote learning.

Underperforming districts prioritize students who fall in the lower bands of performance. Strategies, such as response to intervention (RTI), target students who underperform in bands below proficiency. Educators focus to bring students at these low achieving levels to a level commensurate with their higher achieving peers. Such focus intentionally addresses the academic gap that can continue to grow if students' academic weaknesses are not addressed.

Much of the supplemental resources in a district are poured into programs, support staff, and strategies targeting students in the lower bands of performance. Very little attention is paid to students who are excelling and identified as talented and gifted assisting in their academic growth and promise. Is this possibly one way districts are addressing the widening achievement gap by limiting how far the outliers of high achievers are outperforming their peers? It is a real injustice when we fail to meet the needs of all our students.

At the beginning of the twenty-first century, there was a growing movement to personalize student learning, to create a personal learning experience specifically tailored to the students' level, pace, and learning style. This would require individualized planning for each student that is more engaging, intentional, and appropriate. Curriculum becomes adaptable to the student rather than the student adjusting to the curriculum, better meeting students where they are on the spectrum of learning.

As we push through to the other side of Covid-19, there is an opportunity to utilize personalized learning plans to address the individual needs of each student rather than grouping them in bands of high, low, and middle achievers or chronological age. Media reports revealed the condition of learning during the pandemic and the amount of slippage or learning loss that has occurred. But, there are some students who are excelling with this digital mode of instruction and learning.

Students that are excelling are taking control of their learning, pacing, and depth. Fewer distractions no longer deter students; they are able to engage themselves at their own convenience and readiness. Quantitatively, learning loss happens in students over the summer regardless of their neighborhood or address. Students of color in low poverty areas tend to show a greater loss.

All emphases on collaboration, inquiry, discovery, and social graces have been placed in abeyance as we learn better ways to socially isolate children during instruction. What is evident is the progression of some children in obtaining grade-level standards while others are regressing in their progress.

Analysis conducted by the Center on Reinventing Public Education found that students living in or near low poverty areas were more likely to participate in a remote instructional model while peers in higher income brackets may participate in hybrid or in-person learning. Mainly this may be due to the health of the buildings, air ventilation, staffing, and appropriate space for social distancing.[1] Efforts to meet the learning loss varied across the nation, but it is something that cannot be ignored. Students who were already academically behind are now struggling to recover from loss of time, maintain and learn new content. Inadvertently, it has become a never-ending cycle of catch up. Without the foundations of literacy and other key concepts, these months of loss will never be reclaimed.

District's approach to the recovery of learning loss during Covid-19 varies. Models are not independent of financial constraints to meet students' needs. Some districts have decided to use a looping model, where student's last year's teacher traveled with their students to the next grade to continue teaching the curriculum and capture any gaps that may have occurred. This model allows a broadened perspective on covering the curriculum in a space of time disregarding grade-level limitations. Instruction is focused on mastery of content prior to progressing to the next grade level and curricular standards.

Other districts extended the school year by returning early or adding additional days either at the start or end of the school year. This time is to be used to teach the remainder of the former year's curriculum prior to starting the next grade's curricular standards. Many districts are anticipating the loss of time on learning and are incorporating learning hubs, summer programming, and tutoring models to assist students.

TEXTBOX 11.1

Educational system's rigid structure allows very little room for creative solutions.

Educational system's rigid structure allows very little room for creative solutions. We consistently try to fit the traditional framework into any opportune time for restructuring. Even with the use of technology, online learning still confines students to the scheduled structure, class time, attendance, participation at the assigned time, and assessment. We are trying to place new wine in old wineskins.

SECTION 3: CULTIVATING THE PRISON PIPELINE

Schools have been a great resource for feeding the prison pipeline by funneling children out of the public education system into the juvenile and criminal justice system. Cohorts of children with common factors such as learning disabilities, poverty, and members of the foster system are intentionally isolated, punished, and forced out of the education system into the justice system. High targets are males, students with disabilities, and students of color.

Research shows that children who struggle to read in first grade are 88 percent more likely to struggle in fourth grade. And those who struggle in fourth grade are four times more likely to drop out of school. Illiteracy is a significant characteristic of those who interact with the court system. Especially juveniles, 85 percent are deemed functionally illiterate and 60 percent of the nation's inmates are illiterate (Zoukis 2017).

Both the Children Defense Fund and American Civil Liberties Union (ACLU) acknowledge the school-to-prison pipeline.[2] Public schools' policies, such as zero-tolerance policies that criminalize minor infractions of school rules, become introductory doorways of juveniles into the criminal justice system. Learning disabilities, poverty, abuse, and neglect are other factors that steer children into the juvenile justice system. Students of color are arrested disproportionately while black males, in particular, are at a higher risk. They are three times more likely to be arrested at school than their white counterparts.[3]

Statistics demonstrating the number of children tracked into the prison pipeline would astound you. This is a telling number of whether our schools are truly effective, but we have failed to meet the educational, social, emotional, and psychological needs of these children. Isolation causes disengagement further leading to drop out. How did schools become cisterns?

Aggressively addressing discipline in school, schools went straight to policies and regulations that reflected zero-tolerance. Minor infractions in school rules lead to criminal arrests. School-based arrest begins a fast-track record to criminalization for our youth. Disciplinary matters become a non-ending cycle of repeated time out of school due to suspensions or expulsions, pushing the student further behind in their learning even though the district is legally responsible for continued education.

Realizing the harm the educational system was doing, some districts look to alternatives to discipline that would not result in the juvenile court system.

Vignette: Alternatives to the Juvenile Court System

District 2 uniquely addressed concerns with isolating, punishing, and forcing out students from the respective systems. This district had an extremely high dropout rate for their population. At a given time it was 12 percent higher than any other district in the state and higher than the national average. It was truly a major concern for the community and the board of education.

With the assistance of the mayor and the court system, the school district ran an alternative program for students, with smaller class sizes, district curriculum, vocational opportunities, and numerous support staff to assist with the social-emotional aspect of learning. Of course, this only addressed a small cohort of students, but the adult education program would draw many students back into the classrooms by offering day and night classes.

Employing a second strategy, administrators at the middle and high school level worked together to provide better transitioning from the middle level, targeting students who reflected identified traits of potential dropouts, for instance, those who had poor attendance, retention, underperforming on district assessments, and disciplinary issues.

A summer seminar program was provided prior to the start of school. Students met their teachers, and guidance counselors were able to navigate the school building. As the school year began, students were placed into small cohorts that traveled together for core academic classes. Within their daily schedule, time was provided for study and career planning with peer tutors to assist students with their assignments. A computerized literacy program was also available to assist students who were not yet reading on grade level.

Each student was assigned teacher mentors to assist throughout their first year at the high school. The purpose of targeting students entering ninth grade was a result of analyzing district data and reviewing research. This is the grade when most systems begin to lose students. Course work becomes so challenging that without a solid foundation in literacy, mathematics, writing, and comprehension, students become overwhelmed.

The most important strategy the district employed that addressed dropout and disciplinary issues was changes made to policies and regulations regarding discipline. Staff was trained and implemented restorative practices to keep students in school and to eliminate the high numbers of out-of-school suspensions and expulsions.

Schools limited the number of calls to the police and addressed issues in-house when they could. Some discipline matters were reviewed by a body of students serving as peer mediators to determine outcome and recompense. In many cases, students were asked to give back to the community, especially if it was vandalism. These strategies were done to address the dropout rate, deter students from criminalization, and address the needs of the children in the community.

An enduring obstacle for educators to contend with is to prevent schools from being empty cisterns, holding cells that imprison potential. By targeting our literacy programs, regulations, and policies, these are possible saving graces for our children.

TPQ

1) When developing a budget, how would you equitably distribute resources to address the needs of all children in the district?
2) What is necessary to provide personalized learning to students? How would this benefit all levels of students' performance?
3) How have schools been a source for funneling students into the criminal justice system? What can be done to reverse the negative effects of schooling on these children?

CHAPTER KEY IDEAS

1. Schools for some children have become containment receptacles that either hold back students from academic progress and/or funnel them into the prison pipeline.
2. Current mass education model is prevalently focusing teaching to the lower level often leaving the middle and higher levels with limited support.

NOTES

1. Bethany Gross and Alice Opalka, "As Many School Districts Reopen Virtually, the Opportunity Gap Widens for Students Living in Poverty." (2020) Center on Reinventing Public Education.
2. American Civil Liberties Union (ACLU)—www.aclu.org
   Children Defense Fund—www.childrendefense.org
   http:/www.ocrdata.ed.gove/downloads/crocschool—discipline
3. Education Week Policing America's Schools: an Education Week Analysis. (2017) www.edweek.org/which-students-are-arrested-most-in-school-u-s-data-by-school#/overview
   PBS News Hour (2017) "Analysis Reveals Racial Disparities in School Arrests." www.pbs.org/newshour/education/Analysis reveals racial disparities in school arrests | PBS NewsHour

Chapter 12

Workforce and Talent Development

Your workforce is your most valuable asset. The knowledge and skills they have represent the fuel that drives the engine of business—and you can leverage that knowledge.

—Harvey Mackay

SECTION 1: PREPARING STUDENTS FOR THE FUTURE

Educators have the heavy burden of preparing young people for their future and the future workforce. Unlike in past centuries, we really have no idea what tomorrow's workforce will look like. We can prophetically predict that many of the jobs will be high-tech jobs, requiring those twenty-first-century skill sets mentioned earlier. Most of the manual and labor-intensive jobs will move to automation.

If we can take a play out of the playbook of the agricultural age to the industrial age, each age pushes the other aside. We are currently moving away from mass production, our political party structure is being challenged, our country as a democracy is being challenged, and our position on the world stage is uncertain. What happens when everything is automated? What happens to the educational system as we know it?

Stuck in tradition, the past education system has always characteristically looked like its present. This hiccup of Covid-19 has forced us to adopt new models of teaching our students and giving parents a choice of how the delivery occurs. However, we are still trying to fit an old framework into something new in this current season of uncertainty. Yet, we must still prepare our students for the future workforce.

Failing to prepare students for careers, vocations, and positions that in many respects haven't been created potentially breeds increased poverty. Replenishing the workforce in local towns through changing the educational focus into future trends is critical. It is a hope that the education system is preparing students to be productive and competitive in an abstract, changing, diverse global world that we cannot mimic, but must focus on skills that make our students advantageous.

Workforce development in this day and age is focused on four areas:

1) Aging of the workforce and replacement
2) Diversification of the workforce
3) Flexibility of the workforce
4) Changes in training and development needs

So the antithesis for schools is to ask the question, are we preparing students to replace the retiring workforce, to deal with an increasingly diverse society, to adopt flexibility in workday, and to inculcate the importance of continuing education for further development and advancement?

Over the past decade, the integration of Common Core and career and college readiness described our ultimate goal for students. This is evident in rigorous standards for English Language Arts and mathematics. Increased vigilance on career readiness has increased the technical and vocational classes offered at the traditional comprehensive high school as we earnestly try to prepare students to be viable productive workers. Not everyone is going to college.

Developing the talent of our future workforce should focus on spheres of creativity and innovation being cognizant that artificial intelligence (AI) is and will replace many of the jobs, careers, and professions as we know them. For instance, there is no coincidence in the prioritization of STEM/STEAM in our schools. Being proficient in the skill sets of science, technology, engineering, art, and math, or the collaboration of the fields together, will lead to success in navigating a new age of culture and technology, leading to readiness for the workforce.

TEXTBOX 12.1

Developing the talent of our future workforce should focus on spheres of creativity and innovation.

A return on investment in our children should result in a prepared workforce for the local community and our nation as a whole. We sow and are able to reap! This would be a win-win, but there must be collaboration with local governance, community, and the schools to write a vision that encompasses goals with the future returns. Investment in the community is pivotal to keeping a young workforce in a viable position to create new jobs but to also replace those who are retiring.

What draws young energetic people to a community? What sustains and retains them so that they establish themselves? And reinvest where they live? Answers to these questions are necessary for development and growth. Strong communities are able to sustain themselves through redirection of their culture, values, economics, and growth. Those that are stagnate allow nostalgia to be the driving force of decision-making and are dying or collecting a population with no drive for thought and innovation but are reliant on social services to meet their needs.

TEXTBOX 12.2

Strong communities are able to sustain themselves through redirection of their culture, values, economics, and growth.

Workforce and economic development are two concepts that go hand-in-hand. The economy cannot grow unless there are able bodies, products, and opportunities for workers. This comes with the development of products, resources, and the intellect to develop new products, programs, devices, and systems that go beyond just efficiency but includes an improved design concept for either leisure or need.

Yet as our nation is in and out of recession, less and less of our young people are achieving the American dream of upward mobility. Uncertainty and greater insecurity in our schools for meeting the demands of the workforce have bred contempt for the purpose of mass education and its ever-increasing cost.

Culturally, the education system as an institution is so behind the cultural shifts that have occurred in every other institutions or industries. Cultural shifts occur every three to five years. An individual from the 1800s would have no problems recognizing a classroom with ease—four walls, a central focus whiteboard (black to green to white), desk, and groups of students in one room focused on the same lesson.

If we had a major cultural shift, students would be learning in diverse environments and virtually, multiple lessons occurring in one space, interactions with students across the globe for discussion and debate. It is the real-life application through project-based learning with actual outcomes that affect a changing community. Schools would no longer be defined as a building confined by walls but any acceptable environment, where students are engaged and are actively learning through the application of their knowledge. Then schools would become true places of learning and intellectual prowess.

As cultural shifts take place in other institutions outside of education, we seem to bear the responsibility of assuring the understanding, enforcement, tolerance, and acceptance of that change. We become the vehicle of change without changing ourselves. We just continue to pile on responsibilities without removing or completing an agenda. Our responsibilities extend to the social mores of the culture, such as: imposing the new definition of family, gender neutrality and enculturation, addictions and wellness, sexual preference and acceptance, self-esteem and self-image, and harassment and bullying. Educators just want to teach their subjects!

Vignette: Preparing Students for the Workforce

Part of reform initiatives was for schools to rethink their current instruction model and pedagogical approach by birthing a new construct that specifically addresses the achievement gaps identified in schools. Many state departments of education developed models of accountability that progressively identified the performance of schools and districts based upon granular areas of academic performance, attendance, discipline, graduation rate, and dropout rate. The list of factors ranking districts has expanded, variables dependent upon what the state deems relevant as an indicator for performance and a measure of growth.

One reform model that many schools used focused on thematic academies that centered on a central theme aligned with specific professions. For instance, district 2 was ripe with opportunities surrounding this port city in the area of marine biology, oceanography, and ocean engineering. Partnerships with outside agencies that included the Undersea Naval Reserve allowed for the creation of rich programming centered on marine life, engineering for sea exploration, global climate change, and the effects on the earth's oceans.

At the high school, directed by the science department head, a group of teachers representing cross-content areas collaboratively worked together drafting a STEM program around engineering and oceanography. The program tapped into the resources and already established partnerships. It would also serve as a receiver school for those students wanting to continue from the marine biology program, one of the thematic magnet schools in the district. The whole premise of thematic schools was to establish programs not only pertaining to student interest but in direct connection to careers, occupations, and vocations.

This program was innovatively developed, received the backing of the superintendent, the school council, and the state department of education but had to press through the building administration and union for support. It was a radically different model that would require changes in scheduling, facility usage, smaller class size, and additional staffing to accommodate the smaller class size.

District 3 approached career readiness differently by providing alternative ways for students to engage in vocational courses while attending their comprehensive school. With the help of partnerships with postsecondary institutions and local agencies, students were able to prepare for occupational careers in the areas of law enforcement, fire, automotive, and allied health. These opportunities included coursework, apprenticeships, and internships. Opportunities such as this provide students with authentic hands-on experiences and skills necessary for today and tomorrow's workforce.

Even in the changing age, these types of experiences are relevant in preparing students for a broad spectrum of jobs that will require technology, critical thinking, and creativity. Therefore, coursework and extracurricular opportunities must build on larger concepts and encourage students to think outside the box.

Our world is no longer about concrete problem-solving, but workers must have the capacity to think in the abstract. There are foundational basics that students need to know, but the most important preparation we can give students is to cultivate a desire to think for deeper understanding, make decisions based upon sound evidence, apply their knowledge, and be creative. These are areas that standardized tests rarely assess.

SECTION 2: GLOBALIZATION—INTERDEPENDENT, INTERCONNECTED, AND COMPETITIVE

As our world becomes more interconnected, interdependent, and technologically dependent, it is imperative that we train our students to be competitive and creative in this environment and to decipher through the intensive amount of information discerning what is relevant, true, and helpful. This also means we must have a workforce that is tech-savvy and creative enough to weave twenty-first-century skill sets into the framework of the curriculum so that what students are learning is applicable to the future needs of students when they enter the workforce.

TEXTBOX 12.3

Globalization

Globalization and preparing our students to interact with diversity and to be competitive for the future workforce is important, Covid-19 certainly created alternate experiences for different people of which people fit into one of two economic camps. In the first group, the members are able to work remotely, have predominantly higher levels of education, and white-collar jobs with internet access, and were relatively unscathed by the economic impacts of the pandemic.

In the other camp, people were required to work in unsafe work environments with the general public, may have been laid off, were not allowed to work remotely, and suffered severe economic and health consequences. One key barrier for each group was their level of education and cultural competencies in dealing with customers from afar, whether they were fellow Americans or people living in other countries.

One's education and the curriculum they learned through were then key indicators of future success in the pre-pandemic world. People either had the wherewithal to have a white-collar job or were relegated to the storefronts, shops, and restaurants where no education was required.

Globalization requires the education and understanding of cultural competencies in order to be successful. Without that education, barriers arise to true economic success. Schools can become cultivars of the Prison Pipeline if the curriculum is not good enough, and if it does not include learning about cultural competencies. An excellent curriculum filled with the avant-garde understandings of a globalized world provides students with richer experiences such as international travel which are an eye-opener for the students as they come to know other cultures and how to be "with it" in the new culture and environment.

On the contrary, a mediocre curriculum will just reinforce expectations and habits that thwart further development and raise barriers to learn about cultural competencies, thus providing a pipeline to prison for some. That's why an excellent curriculum is essential in opening doors to economic viability.

For any educational leader, we have daunting tasks and pressures for our students to excel, for the outcomes will dictate who gets what in the future.

Thomas Danehy, Ed.D.
Executive Director

Globalization erases the distance of nations separated by expansive land masses and water and has connected us to each other within nanoseconds. We can interact both socially and virtually with people from other countries using smart Intel devices. This removes one of the most difficult barriers of communication, the second is language. Well, there is an AP for that.

Having access to so much information can be overwhelming. If we focus on the social trends, cognition, soft skills, diversity, citizenship, decision-making, and more, it gives pause to what truly is important for students to learn. Being overwhelmed is not a justification for ineffective instruction. However, it does make one consider what is important to know.

The United States is uniquely different from most nations because of its diversity, a melting pot of many different cultures. We are not homogenous but quite heterogeneous. Because of our uniqueness, a one-way model is not effective or sufficient for all students. This is to our detriment because "what is best for one child may not necessarily be best for another."

Cultural differences should be considered as a means to engage students rather than marginalize them. Not all schools have learned the best recipe to develop the cultural proficiencies to engage all cultures in the school community. This is more than just celebrating multicultural days and observances.

With most importance, the educational focus is on both cognitive and noncognitive skills. These cognitive skills are deciphering, application, synthesizing, problem-solving, and basic knowledge in which one can deepen understanding. And the noncognitive or social-emotional skills are interacting, living, and working with people from different cultures and countries; understanding of what community, humanity, and citizenship means; how each of these factors relates on a global scale; and how human decision-making can impact the lives of individuals in and throughout the world.

The following vignette shows the importance of embracing communities across the globe to celebrate the various cultures that are within the local community. This project showed the value of collaboration as local education agencies, foreign education agencies, higher education agencies, governments, civic and community groups in coming together produced benefits beyond the classroom.

District 2—The Cape Verde Project

In the fall of 2008, a group of community members invited the superintendent to a social outing to introduce her to key members of the Cape Verdean community. What was birthed out of this fellowship was a concern and need to include, celebrate, and recognize their culture in the schools, as the district's population was more than 25 percent of Cape Verdean. With the help of these community leaders, along with a newly hired principal of Cape Verdean descent and teachers in the district, the Cape Verdean project was developed and implemented.

This team of community members and educators made connections to two major schools on the islands of Sao Filipe and Santa Cruz. First, the project's overarching purpose was to truly focus on global education, awareness, and citizenship by connecting students to their history and cultural heritage. Second, the project was to explore pressing issues around education and community development through cross-cultural exchange.

Collaboratively, the team worked directly with students, teachers, and the community to discuss and understand how human decisions can directly impact the lives of individuals in multiple countries. The goal was to prepare students for work and civic roles in a globalized environment. A global friendship was developed with the country's minister of education, administrators, and teachers that resulted in exchanged visits for professional development.

Students at the elementary level established pen pals and video diaries to share lessons with their peers across the ocean. At the middle and high school level with the support and networking of a local college (now university), a forum was conducted through video conferencing discussing topics such as the impact of human decision-making on economic development, agriculture and the use of hydroponics in arid regions, and the diaspora and current life on the islands. Students discussed social concerns that included illiteracy, conflict, violence, joblessness, health, and poverty.

This project and the relationships forged throughout not only strengthened the school district's relationship with the families and community but helped the district to better meet the needs of the increasing population of students emigrating from this country to the city. The district's immersion programs developed stronger practices to meet cultural barriers, language differences, and strategies to assist with acculturation.

Student outcomes from this project included an appreciation of culture and heritage, global awareness, building confidence and character, fostering humanity, expanding educational opportunities outside the classroom, and preparing students to commensurate and interact with people of diverse backgrounds. Exchanges included video diaries on topics selected by students, pen pals, and student and teacher exchanges.

It is critical to prepare young people for the future; skill requirements are changing quickly and vastly. We have made the shift from the industrial model of producing a product to an information-intensive economy. Production jobs that remain require higher-level skills, for instance, manufacturing and automotive fields require a workforce with mental acuity, math and science skills. Many of US jobs are tied to exports, and this is expected to expand.

Complexity of global integration of economies and competition for industries, high skills, and high-wage jobs is intensifying and will increasingly intensify as countries reposition themselves, and superpowers are renamed.

Automation has replaced the fearful outsourcing of low-skilled, low-wage jobs, and, with the help of technology, distance is no longer a barrier. Because of this, we may now find that we are in direct competition with workers from all over the world. Educators must prepare our children to be viable workers with comparable skills.

Three critical questions we must ask of our schools and the curriculum that we implement. How will our interchanges move our students to be more globally aware? What is the evidence that demonstrates that our students are proficient global citizens? Are we preparing our students to be competitive within the global arena?

With optimism, if we treat schools as receptacles full of potential and harness this potential in such a transformative way, we can begin to see productive pools that benefit the community that surrounds it. This comes by investing in schools with future forward thinking that can project the future environment students will be working in.

It brings to mind traditional examples of how communities aligned their curriculum based on the needs of their community, such as traditional examples of farming communities that focused their curriculum on agriculture or seashore communities on marine biology or technology giants' implementation of STEM and coding. Truly investing in students as the human capital of tomorrow, with their capacity to think, produce and flourish.

Pessimistically, schools that fail to recognize the changing world around them by closing their eyes to the ever-encroaching progress of globalization are committing a disservice in preparing their youth for what is next in the future world. Empty cisterns can be made into prisons, but broken cisterns are good for nothing. They cannot hold anything nor produce.

TPQ

1) What interchanges are necessary and how will these interchanges move students to be more globally aware?
2) What evidence demonstrates students are proficient global citizens? What should schools do to ensure proficiency?
3) Is the present-day educational system preparing students to be competitive within the global area? Why or why not?

CHAPTER KEY IDEAS

1. The needs of the future workforce are predicated on the changing landscape of technology and the greater use of AI. At best, we can prepare students with twenty-first-century skills to assist them in navigating this dynamic change.

2. Community partnerships can assist in sustaining economic growth within their communities by driving innovation within the schools.
3. Students must be prepared to participate and compete in the changing global economy by possessing both cognitive and noncognitive skills that adapt to the expansive needs of a global community.

Part 6

BREAKING AND FILLING

Chapter 13

Breaking the Nets, Filling the Trenches, Sinkholes, and Cisterns

If you have built castles in the air, your work need not be lost; that is where they should be. Now put foundations under them.
—Henry David Thoreau

SECTION 1: VISUALIZING THE PERFECT EDUCATIONAL UTOPIA

Can we overcome the obstacles and yield to the possibilities that prevail when the nets are broken, trenches ever widening into chasms, sinkholes as abysses, and cisterns filled? Even returning to the basic rudimentary functionality of schooling would be a disservice. Can we break nets holding students and release students to experience situations that allow them to excel and grow to their potential? Can we stop limiting students' growth through determining their capacity based upon grade level, poverty status, color of their skin, gender, and language or lingual ability?

> **TEXTBOX 13.1**
>
> Can we break nets that are demographic in nature that are known to place limits on students' growth and progress? Such demographic factors include age, poverty status, skin color, gender, and language or lingual ability.

Responding to such paradigm shifts would require us to move away from the one size-fits-all model, fixed and inflexible schedules, chronological age standards, four-walled classrooms, and desks in rows. At this point in history, we are facing a pandemic that has shut down all of our social systems, including education. The educational system has responded with a band-aide of distance learning. Inconsistency of curricular work, grading, and inequities of access arise in the rollout of the make-shift home classroom.

Although we are in a season of transition in the wake of a pandemic, we are still contending with the same problems previous to the pandemic. What now, since the everyday norm has been interrupted? Do we return to the norm or do we take advantage of the opportunity to start from scratch? The coronavirus pandemic has us asking questions, but these questions are how to return to normalcy rather than moving forward. We have a window of opportunity to reset the educational system.

In general, a system is defined as an organization of interrelated and interdependent parts that somehow unify all those parts to bring accord. The educational system is no different. It is the complexities and hierarchies of these parts that cause conflict within relationships. Because of this, systems, in reality, are never stable and subject to scrutiny and failure.

Yet, research shows that effective school systems focus on five areas to achieve an educational utopia or as close to achieving an ideal state of what a "good" education should attain. Within these areas, trusting relationships and accountability are pivotal for meeting and measuring goals, collaboration among stakeholders, and guidance and direction for the district's future.

The five areas that are characteristic of an effective school system include: (1) a rigorous curriculum that is vertically aligned and focusing on twenty-first-century skills, (2) an embedded accountability model that involves every aspect of the system, (3) leadership that blends both managerial and instructional approaches to leading, (4) partnership with parents and the community, and (5) forward thinking.

SECTION 2: RIGOROUS CURRICULUM EMBEDDING TWENTY-FIRST-CENTURY SKILLS

Rigor is a qualifying word often used to describe the strength of a district's curriculum, difficulty of the course work, the level of the courses offered, and what the teacher requires of the student. Rigor also quantifies the austerity or inflexibility of the curriculum. However, an effective curriculum is one in which students are required to think critically and to problem-solve by applying foundational knowledge to new experiences.

Rigor demands high expectations of active use of core knowledge accountable talk, construction of understanding, and meaning through interactions with others or stimuli. Such demands come from the instructional practices or pedagogy of the teacher.

Districts that build their teacher workforce with teachers of this caliber and continuously provide professional opportunities for teachers' growth see a direct impact on students' academic achievement and performance. High-performing districts move students from codependence to independence. Students exhibit a very different level of maturity and self-management. Perceivably there is a different environment for underperforming districts. Students are more reliant on the teacher to thrive. Visibly a codependency is evident in the way students' days are structured and a greater reliance on the teacher for transitions.

Districts that have adopted the twenty-first-century skillset embed critical thinking, creativity, collaboration, communication, literacy (informational, media, and technical), flexibility, and leadership. Such an approach is imitative within the teachers' instructional practices preparing students to be workforce ready for the informational age. Rigor also encapsulates a sense of expectation for students' behavior.

Vignette: A Tale of Two School Districts

High-performing schools exhibit distinct common characteristics. School environment and culture are cohesive and strong where relationships among the different strata are respectful, reverent, and trusting. Leadership is transparent and within the mores of the community, exhibiting behaviors of servanthood, sharing in the work of the district. There is a singular mission of meeting students' needs and fostering a strong academic focus for every child. This shared mission produces a culture of accountability from the central office to the school building.

Staff are well qualified and are hired based upon specific profiles that match the culture and expectations of the district, yielding high performance. Professional development and opportunities are provided to the staff to continue their professionalism and strengthen their craft. They conduct and engage in action research to improve their instructional strategy, student engagement and differentiation, and student learning. Staff also collaborates in lesson planning and assessment. A common language is spoken throughout the district, and guiding principles are in practice that dictates behaviors and actions.

Students exhibit a level of maturity and independence in their learning; they take ownership and responsibility for their learning and execute executive functioning. Learning is a priority and a necessity. This same value is a mantra of the entire community and is reinforced throughout the mindset of the community. Families and community members are engaged and involved through continuing the learning at home, partnering with schools, and serving as a resource.

Walking down the hallway in any of the district's schools, an observer would see the flow of routines that are intermingled with interactions of adults and students that demonstrate respect. Behaviors are well managed by the students and staff participating in the school community.

Peering into the classroom, students are working collaboratively together to solve a problem. Some students are engaged in deep conversations about the work at hand while some are leading and directing the learning while the teacher facilitates. Students are creating and applying core foundational knowledge.

Communication is transparent and even though there is a hierarchy within the organizational structure, there is shared responsibility in leadership as it flows through the chain of command. Because of this transparency, members of the organization feel free to take the risk, invest, and care for one another's needs such as esteem, value, and respect.

Crossing over to a second district, a very different picture is painted. As an observer walking into any of the schools, the starkness of the culture is evident. Leadership, the superintendent, is rarely seen, and school building leadership as well. School building leadership is hindered by suppressing the numerous parent and community complaints and discipline of students.

Teachers' classroom doors are closed and there is no sharing of lessons or strategies to improve students' understanding. There is animosity among the staff and a sense of competitiveness of performance in moving up the hierarchy. Many of the teachers appear to be in survival mode and struggling to thrive in the environment. An overwhelming feeling of angst is triggered by behaviors of students, staff, leadership, and parents.

Students are disengaged or inattentive to the lesson and easily are distracted by the behaviors of others around them. Schoolwork is remedial or on the low level of Bloom's taxonomy as worksheets and now digitized worksheets fill students with busy work and very little deeper understanding. The community devalues the system by speaking negatively of it, and very few partnerships are welcomed.

There are very stark differences in the two districts, but very real impacts on students learning and success, as well as staff morale and retention. The former district would be qualified as rigorous while the latter as mediocre. Communality or shared sense of purpose among the district's community has a driven pursuit of excellence. Emotionally, the second district may too desire excellence for their students but are trapped in low expectations and are challenged to break the cycle.

SECTION 3: ACCOUNTABILITY

Accountability extends far beyond assessing students and monitoring their progress. Effective districts have an accountability plan that assesses every area of the system to assure that there is veracity, quantifiable progress, and intentionality of attaining the vision, mission, and goals of the district. It becomes the framework or scaffolding that aligns experiences, beliefs, and actions with desired results.

Transparency attaches to accountability. Nothing is hidden and conversations include reality about the needs of the schools and children within the community. Every area of school management should have well-established quantifiers that give reliability and validity to organizational structure, decision-making, and progress.

SECTION 4: LEADERSHIP

Finding "the right fit" is like pieces to a puzzle. Most districts prefer different criteria when selecting a leader for their district. Some look at personality, integrity, malleability, work history, physical characteristics, gender, and even political party affiliation. Others search for a specific strength to compensate for what is currently lacking in the district. Whatever the preference, the leader needs to have a meld of managerial, instructional, and transformative leadership styles.

TEXTBOX 13.2

Leadership

Maximizing learning as measured by student outcomes is the focus of education in our schools. After the quality of teachers, the second most important leverage strategy is leadership. Educational leaders like principals and administrators create the conditions for teachers to succeed with their students and their learning in the classroom. Leaders are critical for a successful school system. The question becomes what type of leader is needed in school districts to avoid sinkholes that perpetuate the status quo among teachers and staff. How do we create school districts that focus on what is best for students and not for adults?

There are three "buckets" of leadership skills that need to be tools for any principal or administrator: instructional, managerial, and political. Administrators need to have a level of knowledge and master of skills in each one of the three areas. The level of mastery within each area may vary depending on the context of the position (assistant principal, supervisor of special education, etc.).

However, every successful administrator must have a minimum level of mastery within an area, because you cannot make managerial decisions without instructional knowledge, and you cannot make instructional decisions without understanding the political (or public relations) of a school district.

There are three distinct areas of leadership that all administrators must have a minimum mastery of skills. Instructional leadership is the mastery of teaching and learning principles that benefit all students' education. Managerial leadership is creating systems and structures to provide organizational coherence for all district functions. Political leadership or understanding the public relations frame reminds administrators about the context of their school and how the community stakeholders would respond. These three areas of leadership and their skills are critical for successful administrators.

Having interviewed over 1,000 applicants for school leadership positions, I look for these three "buckets" of skills to find the best candidate for an administrative position. In a review of the last fifteen years, the administrators who have successfully mastered these three areas have been recognized as "Principal of the Year" and role models to emulate.

Joseph P. Macary, Ed.D.
Superintendent of Schools

Regardless of how transformative one's leadership practices are, effective leaders must still be able to manage the workforce. It is necessary to engage the staff and ensure that they have the necessary skills for the work that is assigned. An effective leader must be able to think strategically in planning for the future of the district, invest in human capital, and control resources with the overall goal of achieving the mission and vision of the district.

By sustaining, retaining, growing, and developing staff, high-performing school districts invest in their teachers through opportunities for professional growth, development, career movement, and incentives. Value of investment is to see teachers as assets that are indispensable. Quality teachers are pivotal to student achievement. Teachers who are highly committed to their art are continuously developing, properly paid, and are connected to a supportive network of peers.

Willing to follow the leader's ability, the school community must trust in the leader's capacity to lead. But, leadership is restricted by the ability, resources, and willingness of the people who surround the leader. Lack of cohesion between leadership and the school community impacts the effectiveness of the leadership and results in divisiveness and underperformance.

SECTION 5: PARTNERSHIPS AND FORWARD THINKING

Informational age is triggering thinking beyond the present horizon. Schools should not want to be left behind. We want to produce a product, no scratch that! We want students ready to be competitive in a globally diverse environment.

Organizational structures that work well are inclusive of trusting partnerships and relationships. Such relationships are forged by identifying roles and responsibilities, following principles of management, providing reciprocity between management and staff, and having a common mission with actionable goals reflective of the vision. Trusting partnerships are where "stabbing me in the back" is not allowed or tolerated within the community of stakeholders. Offenses are forgiven and retaliation or vindication is not the way of life.

Substantially good things come out of partnerships, but they must be commensal. That is why trusting relationships are crucial. Districts that harness the resources around them and work alongside families find stronger support for programs and the direction the district is progressing toward.

Separation, isolation, and despair in relationships are caused by a spirit of offense and put people on the defense. Results of offense produce an atmosphere of low morale, low innovation, fear, and distrust. When an organization functions effectively, there is an expectation of trust, assurance of safety in risk taking for innovation, and a belief in the mission of the organization. It becomes a body that is one, diverse in other ways, but stands together when it comes to the good of the children. Beliefs, values, and expectations should be in alignment with the journey of strengthening the effectiveness of a school district.

So how do we become one or united, when we are so diverse in both our physical being and thinking? Diversity could breed advantages because it births new ways of thinking, but it also causes divisiveness. Individuals, who impart stereotypical biases and prejudices about other people, stir the waters of contention. When beliefs about others are contingent on one's race, gender, ethnicity, or age, it affects one's ability to trust and build relationships and impedes the work of the organization.

Most times these issues are not confronted and become buried until a decision or policy causes beliefs to rise to the surface creating an environment that becomes tense or even hostile, in some cases dealing with internal relational issues rather than helping the needs of the children. But these same internal issues impact the relationship the schools have with the community in which it serves.

However, the advantage of having a diverse workforce brings multiple voices to the table, contributing different perspectives to problem-solving, planning, and decision-making. An organization has to be willing to recognize and value the difference of their workforce and use it to their advantage in the operation and delivery of service to their community. Also, the organization should reflect the population in which it serves. That includes the commitment to developing and implementing policies and practices that engender participation and inclusion of all voices.

Internally, trusting partnerships are built from identified roles and responsibilities of each party that has entered the partnership; the same is for partnerships that are established with bodies outside of the educational system. An agreement or "pact" can be written that clarifies each party's roles and responsibilities.

> **TEXTBOX 13.3**
>
> Internally, trusting partnerships are built from identified roles and responsibilities of each party that has entered the partnership.

Trusting partnerships where there is quid pro quo or symbiotic relationships whereas members of the community are interdependent or mutually benefiting one another is necessary for an organization to work. We briefly talked about mutualism and the bonds it creates within the relationship serving as a bridge in the trench (see chapter 3). Relationships in which only one party benefits many times produce an unstable bond or a rift between parties. Such imbalanced relationships could further leave one member of the partnership feeling disenfranchised and without voice at the decision table. A power struggle ensues.

Questions leaders, along with their school community, should ask are: What partnerships and relationships have we created to benefit the well-being of students? For instance, working with postsecondary institutions, workforce investment groups, the chamber of commerce, nonprofits to name a few. These are the kind of partnerships that better position our students to be successful after high school and more competitive when entering the workforce. And what reciprocity can we give in support of their partnership? Balancing the relationship so that each party benefits.

Building such partnerships is mutually beneficial; for instance, postsecondary institutions can allow students to take college courses prior to completing high school. The benefits are numerous to the student in that they have earned college credit toward a degree, potentially at a lower tuition rate, and challenged themselves with more rigorous content. Potentially completing a degree in less time and utilizing the schoolyear to earn dual credit. Parents have cost savings; the district teacher to student ratio may decline resulting in cost savings in human resources to the district.

Many districts through the assistance of grants or stipulated agreements are able to provide higher education courses to secondary students. Workforce investment and economic development groups can assist and guide what essential skills students will need to be successful after completing schooling. Poll studies indicate what industries will need workers and what jobs will no longer exist due to technology and AI replacement of human labor.

TEXTBOX 13.4

Workforce investment and economic development groups can assist and guide what essential skills our students will need to be successful after completing schooling.

Employing principles of management contributes to a results-oriented organizational culture. By engaging all stakeholders to work toward a single goal by providing collaborative guidance, direction, equity, and stability through the division of work roles and responsibilities, such structure can be intentional in meeting the needs of the population being served.

For instance, high-performing districts invest in their teachers by practices and processes that are developing effectiveness and professionalism. Management ensures that teachers have all the resources they need to be effective, and both management and staff actionably work toward the common mission and goals of the district.

Although we may be diverse and different, we can become unified by focusing on a singular mission and goal. For educators, that is to improve the lives of children by teaching, preparing, and giving them tools to manage and press through the experiences of life.

The individual relationships that make up the whole of the organization focusing on this singular goal of improvement unify the district to travel in a multilinear pattern that is moving in the same direction and convening at a single point of success. Uniformity of purpose is the essential key to navigating the multitudinous layers of hierarchy and structure within the system.

TEXTBOX 13.5

Uniformity of purpose is the essential key to navigating the multitudinous layers of hierarchy and structure within the system.

Unification or unified thinking toward a single goal is independent of one's personal agenda and personal will. Divergent opinions and thoughts must converge at the end of the day around the singular focus drawing all levels of the hierarchy to it. Division of labor gets the work done, but when the efficiency of the division of labor becomes bureaucratic, it detours the work. Diversity of talent among the members of the organization and other stakeholders should be used to the advantage of the organization. Weak relationships impoverish us and prevent us from getting the work done.

TEXTBOX 13.6

Weak relationships impoverish us and prevent us from getting the work done.

Each stratum should discharge results that benefit the whole organization rather than arrows that cause failure. Active cooperation of the strata (all the parts) gives credence to the condition of the organization. This would be a good point to revisit the concept of mutualism discussed in chapter 3. One would think that the organization's desire is for all parts of the organization to benefit and not one part to feel oppressed. Yet an organization that is within internal conflict is a poor teacher of helping students and communities find social cohesion.

So the goal speaks of improvement and the individual players "sounds their own note" to manifest the reality of the goal. Combining the work of the strata produces harmony. All the diversities of operation within a system should represent movement toward the singular goal. The goal not only is the focus but what draws the diversities of operation to it. Do we willfully want to achieve the goal? What interventions are needed to continuously move toward the goal? Is it more dependent upon the relationships (intra and inter) of the strata rather than isolation?

Mission is to denote a single purpose, an honest aim without any mixture of a selfish base. In essence, actuate in the best possible manner by working together in achieving the mission and goals. Instead, nets, trenches, sinkholes, and cisterns are destructive causes that promote self-gain of influence, power, control, and prosperity at the expense of children and the community. These obstacles have become tactile strategies of keeping the entire base from achieving success.

Each stratum has a role and responsibility to discharge with fidelity. If done with unity and integrity toward the mission and goals of the organization, it would yield a learning environment conducive to where every child could excel.

Unification irrespective of differences is a bond of union that goes beyond superficial differences of race, gender, economic status, or opinion. It instinctually pursues means to achieve mission and goal and recoils at those things that cause nets, trenches, sinkholes, and cisterns. Too much unification causes one to think of others' needs more highly than their own. It becomes a cure for envy, jockeying for position and recognition. It makes us consider "what could be" versus the painful reality of "what we are."

TPQ

1) How do we approach the obstacles that limit students' growth and change the narrative that stigmatizes social-economic status, race and ethnicity, gender, and language barriers affects on the academic progress of students?
2) What would an educational reset look like if given the opportunity to restart the educational system?
3) How can a leader change the existing culture of a school district? What factors need to be considered?

CHAPTER KEY IDEA

An effective school system has the following five qualities: a rigorous curriculum, system accountability, a leader that approaches leadership with a blend of both managerial and instructional skills, family and community partnerships, and forward thinking.

Chapter 14

Overcoming the Hierarchy of Power

Power does not corrupt. Fear corrupts . . . perhaps the fear of a loss of power.

—John Steinbeck

SECTION 1: WHAT TO DO?

Power is essential to leadership. Without it, leaders cannot lead. Power provides the capacity to help others to be influential and to be effective in fulfilling the goals of the school district. It has a tendency to make leaders more vulnerable and prone to arrogance, ill will toward others, and despotism. But, power provides a greater opportunity for its expression by removing restraints and consequences. It gives one the freedom to act, uninhibited by parameters, and it allows for innovation.

In a system with hierarchical strata, there are built-in checks and balances to control the power grid of the hierarchy, such as the board of education is the governing body or the superintendent is the manager. Those in authoritative positions can decide to unleash or harness power. For instance, power that is unleashed can be explosive and destructive, causing chaos. Or it can be channeled in such a way that it is controlled through systems, providing something useful.

Issues occur when a power struggle ensues within an organizational structure or system. This weakens the effectiveness of an organization in carrying out its goals and mission (see chapter 7). What occurs is that the most influential state of the hierarchy promotes its agenda. We can see the direct effects of this at the lowest ecological level with the struggle of power between the board of education versus the superintendent, the board of education versus parents, the superintendent versus the administrator, the administrator versus the teacher, and teacher versus the parent.

Politics and power of control over another is a significant obstacle that is a pervasive struggle within the educational system. There are codes and rules of engagement in power struggles usually fortified by position.

But at the macro level, we see the impact of other systems such as family, government, media, business, religion, arts, and entertainment on education. Not one single entity is to blame for the inequities and injustices that occur in schools but it is an amalgamation of many factors as a result of these systems.

Each system has a role to play and exerts its power of influence. These systems are constantly evolving in ideology and agenda, evident in the things that were considered nonacceptable forty years ago are now tolerated, even encouraged. For instance, the family structure has changed in such a way that parents over many policy maneuvers have relinquished their rights to parent their own child. Other systems have weakened the influence of this system.

Parental voices are sounding off with a protest against Covid-19 restrictions, mask mandates, mass vaccination, gender identity, critical race theory, and "woke" culture. They are pushing back against such policies and its future impacts on the next generation's liberties. Parents have been labeled domestic terrorists by the department of justice. This only enhances the friction and power struggle between those appointed to the position of governance and the voice of the people.

Government, a second influential system, is in a chaotic state as we slide from nonpartisan to further left. As a country, we are becoming more liberal and socialistic in our values and thinking. Currently, political parties are greatly divided; it is a power struggle over who rules. Policies and decisions are not necessarily for the good of the people but to destroy agendas of one party over another. This tension and behavior are reflected in the governance and behavior of constituents in our cities and throughout the nation. Many are in fear of losing basic freedoms and liberties.

Media, a third system, plays a major role in that its power comes from telling the story.

The media is an excellent resource for changing the narrative of a situation. But often, the media distorts the narrative and is biased in its storytelling. Most times using sound bites to sensationalize a story impacts how the story is interpreted. Many times the narrative tends to be one-sided.

The media communicates small morsels of information until listeners shape their thinking around what was fed. Changing or directing the narrative disrupts one's thinking yielding a sense of uncertainty. No longer assurance of what is truth. Reiteration of events whether truthful or not is internalized becoming a part of one's thinking. Unfortunately, it results in stereotypes, stigmas, and false beliefs. There are many apt leaders who are unemployed because of the falsities of the airwaves.

Vignette—Tales of the Media

A nonparent community member felt it was her duty to assist the political agenda and forcibly target nonrenewal of the superintendent's contract. She commissioned herself to do an online poll on whether the superintendent should be renewed.

During public comment prior to voting on contract renewal, she spoke of a 400 signed petition that was completed online. She handed a brown envelope over to the board. No one opened, questioned, or investigated it. The media quickly had newsworthy headline using the document. Sad to say, the online petition was signed by people who were residents outside of the community. Some signatures were forged and repeated to make the numbers. The press will never retract the story.

Vignette—Media's Interpretation of Images

A picture is a thousand words. During an exciting board meeting, one of the board members became extremely agitated and vocal over the principals' contract negotiations. His emotional charge was directed toward the principals and their union heads. However, the next day's newspaper caption spins the commentary and crops the photo depicting the outburst as an act toward the superintendent and fails to mention the discussion around the outburst.

Both short vignettes paint a picture of how the storyteller shapes the narrative of what others believe consequential to the reality of what has taken place. The narrative then dictates our response to what has happened as causation to our own perspectives rather than truth. It then manifests in our lives as either perverse or proverbial.

Rejection of another's abilities and capacity, insecurity, involving another's territory, breaking promises, violations, and intentionality to railroad another for no apparent reason but because you can, such behavior causes the less empowered party of the power struggle to turn inward, disconnecting and untrusting in the absence of an authentic partnership. This isolation is dangerous especially when the superintendent is the party that is the one isolated. It inhibits cooperation and often results in retaliation or hostility.

Media is influential by damaging relationships and spinning the narrative. As a system, it has painted a negative image of schools, children, communities, and the professionalism of educators. Business, as the fourth system impacting education is the driving force of what is taught and how it is taught by pushing products to make a profit.

Religion, the fifth system that impacts education is driving the exodus of students out of the public school system to homeschooling or faith-based schools. It is also speaking to some of the policies that are against religious doctrine. What is interesting, this system too is showing great signs of division and divisiveness with doctrine, practice, and principles. But nevertheless, it is impacting our schools.

Arts and entertainment, the last system, projects images of identity. What society perceives as acceptable and what we should strive toward. This has given messages that are contributing to some of those social-emotional problems in which students are coping. Each system is struggling for power and impacts or interplays with other systems.

Reform is not enough, but what is needed is a complete rethinking of how the education system is designed and works. This may be necessary for breaking the nets and leveling the ground for a strong foundation that is strategically positioned and reinforced to prevent trenches, sinkholes, and cisterns.

Breaking the net of the "one" whose portion is fat, the one who catches those who are helpless or oppressed by the system would result in victory and an opportunity to change direction. Power struggles garner power at the expense of others, suppressing others with the advantages they possess.

TEXTBOX 14.1

Power struggles garner power at the expense of others, suppressing others with the advantages they possess.

Many times, the political machine will use divisive issues for political gain or engage in opportunism. This increases their influence over others at the cost of impugning the performance of the district. Likewise, in the educational arena political leaders run on platforms that in effect target an area of education; this drives the results of elections and eventually policies.

By advocating for the helpless and refusing to treat them as one whole "mass" of mediocrity without distinction, educators can begin to change the present landscape of schools. We must also think bigger above the basic needs of our current state of affairs and have a larger eye-view of what the educational system as a whole must become to address the current needs and prepare our students to be successful in the changing world. When we fail to look forward, fix our eyes on what we have been in the past and perseverate on limitations blamed mostly on false viewpoints; it paralyzes transformation or reform efforts.

SECTION 2: A HOUSE IN ORDER CANNOT BE DIVIDED

A foundation is pivotal to any structure maintaining its uprightness, but when there is a crack in the foundation or the structure is built on marshlands, it is bound to eventually sink. So too in the political arena, when political parties clash or people with differing beliefs on governing become divided, the resulting chaos comes with distractions, new harmful laws, injustice, and dysfunction.

What strengthens the foundation of a school district is the need for cohesive relationships; the same can be said on the system's level, the relationship of education to the other six systems. What would cohesion look like? A house that is in order cannot fall.

Using water as an example of cohesion and fluidity, water is a substance that has no defined shape except when frozen. It takes the shape of the container it is in, molding itself into any form its holder allows. Water by gravity flows and seeps its way into places and makes its own pathway. It is significant to life and yet can be a destructive force that alters landscapes and life as we know it.

Structures built near water or on water are subject to the natural forces that interact with water. Foundations of these structures may be challenged, given these structures may sink, tilt, or totally submerge. Land availability and use to build schools in landlocked areas may have districts resort to building on wetlands or even landfills. There are environmental guidelines and safety measures to follow that prevent some of the mishaps that could occur. If not, the structure may be prone to flooding, collapsing through structural failure, and cracking of the foundation reducing the lifespan of the building.

Regardless of following environmental guidelines, there is a risk of building a structure on less than firm ground. We can say the same about building an educational system on less than firm ground. Without a strong foundation, we are subject to sinking. The system becomes subject to the disturbances within and surrounding it.

Districts 1 and 2 both struggled with environmental concerns on their properties. Each district addressed its concerns by lining the waste and creating a border. District 3 had a school that was sinking into the ground as evidenced by the depth and ground fill around the building. These are true concerns that occupied a great deal of time for the administration and board of education to rectify and address the concerns of the school community.

Although real environmental concerns locally and metaphorically, it speaks to the structures that as a bureaucratic system the nation has built over time on an insecure foundation that is no longer meeting the needs of all our students.

Marshy land is constantly adjusting to the disturbances occurring within and surrounding it. It learns to adapt. The educational system as a whole is adjusting to the social mores of the culture that is influenced by other systems as mentioned. It supports or instructs the belief or point of view that is currently acceptable by the majority of society. But, its adaptations over the decades fail to meet the needs of all students, leaving some children unprepared for the present age or the age to come.

Untrusting relationships weaken the foundation of the organization. It is difficult to build trusting relationships when there is insecurity and a risk of harm. Most of us frame our realities around what we interpret from our experiences. But most times, the interpretation comes from a self-centered perspective. For instance, "How does it affect me?"

Yet in healthy relationships, there is confidence in the character and integrity on both sides of the relationship that neither party will be harmed. The more violations of trust and promises, the more difficult it is to repair the broken relationship. Partners set boundaries around another's behavior by limiting interactions and what one will trust another with. Communication becomes less effective when we act out of insecurities; we become less effective.

TEXTBOX 14.2

"Expect Great Things!"

This was the mantra that many of us adopted after I began serving as superintendent in a CT urban district. The idea was to move away from a culture of "We're here in this negative place, what do you expect?" to a recognition of the learning community's value and a new attitude of high expectations.

It was then and remains true today that this particular school system, like many others, has the potential to be great. The issues that forestall reaching their potential often center around politics and, by extension, funding. In the case of this particular district during my tenure, politics (small "p"—think, adult agenda—in addition to big "P") and funding were indeed the obstacles that captured our children.

Superintendents today have a unique opportunity to move the academic performance needle because of the influx of ESSER dollars. Politics, however, can still be the burden that limits progress. Please consider the following as you undertake today's challenges.

After completing various audits cosponsored by the state's department of education, my new administration and supporting community set about the task of developing a comprehensive strategic plan. As district leadership moved toward plan implementation, we determined to partner with the National Urban Alliance (NUA) to carry out culturally responsive professional development for our teachers. Our intention was to roll out this training in a holistic way by including every district school.

We were clear that coherence, consistency, and fidelity were key. Thus, we designed a schedule that would provide all school leaders with overarching training at the outset while phasing each school's staff more deeply into the NUA process over a three-year period. We knew that this work would make a real difference in the lives of our students giving them the confidence to excel as they discovered and pursued their talents and interests. But politics got in the way.

In order to meet the funding requirements to provide the NUA training, we identified Title 1 and any other available dollars but needed additional money in order to realize a total district rollout. So, we turned to business and philanthropic partners for assistance. Here is where the politics raised up!

One leading philanthropic group decided that the NUA work would take too long to reap results. This set off a domino effect where other potential funders followed suit in not responding positively to meet our needs. Was this leading foundation's representative being objective in his decision process?

Did individual foundation and business representatives have an issue with particular NUA personnel? Were external and/or internal representatives off-put by the fact that the NUA was primarily staffed by people of color? Were elected officials or union representatives sabotaging the effort to raise money? What were the adult issues (the politics) that caused potential financial supporters to stand down in their commitment to bolster the strategic plan goals?

As it was, we used the funding we had to manage a partial rollout. In those instances where impacted schools and their principals implemented the NUA training with fidelity, we saw major growth in achievement resulting in student self-actualization as well as outside recognition of the schools' success. I am left to think about the thousands of children captured in the adult nets, unable to access the wonderful opportunities that only some received.

The plan was solid. The NUA training was and is among the best in the country. As compared to other potential training partners, the NUA process takes no longer to manifest results and the costs are competitive. So what was the problem that kept funders from coming on board? I don't suppose we'll ever know the real answers, but you can bet that adult issues, politics, were front and center.

So, what does this mean for you, Ms./Mr. Superintendent, as you pursue your work in this Covid-19, CRT paranoid, ESSER reality? How do you contend with these particular nets of politics and funding? Well, if I had the complete answer, I suppose I'd be on a book/speaking tour. However, I can suggest that you: be aware of these nets, work to build professional, goal-oriented relationships both inside and outside of the organization, apply data to the proposals you assert, and maintain your integrity at every turn.

John J. Ramos, Sr., Ed.D.
President, Equity and Excellence Imperative
Retired Superintendent

TPQ

1) Power, politics, and practice, all three impact the educational system. Define "power" and its importance in "getting things done." How does "power" align with politics and effect actual practices within a district?

CHAPTER KEY IDEAS

1. There are seven systems that impact our world: education, family, government, media, business, religion, and arts and media. Each system interacts and impacts the other by exerting its power of influence.
2. Power struggles garner power at the expense of others, suppressing others with the advantages the power holder possesses.
3. Division that occurs within the hierarchy of education can be addressed by balancing the impact of other systems and strengthening relationships.
4. Over time, adaptations to social mores of the culture to meet societal trends have weakened the foundation of the educational system. The system has failed to meet the needs of all students leaving some unprepared for the present or coming age.

Part 7

DENOUEMENT

Chapter 15

Denouement

Overcoming Obstacles and the Possibilities That Prevail

Our real blessings often appear to us in the shape of pains, losses and disappointments; but let us have patience, and we soon shall see them in their proper figures.

—Joseph Addison

SECTION 1: ENTRY INTO SUPERINTENDENCE

Vignette—An Urban Superintendent's Story

It was the middle of the summer, ambitious, optimistic, quixotic, and full of big ideas; the new superintendent was ready to start the next level of her career. It was a dream of hers to become a school superintendent, culminating her education and final steps in her career. Although not many know the stress and political stakes of the position, she was aware of what was before her and was up for the challenge.

This narrative style vignette is to share with you a superintendent's pathway to becoming an agent of change, her experience as an agent of change in an urban school system that needed repair, the bumpy road she trudged through the metaphorical malaise of nets, sinkholes, trenches, and cisterns, and how she remained resilient as a leader in an era where public education as a system is questioned for its systemic practices.

Young, energetic, and enthusiastic, she embraced the challenge ahead of her. It was a season of change, filled with high expectations of self, expectations from the community in which she served, and expectations from key powers of opposition. Expectations she held for herself were grounded in the hopes of improving the overall climate and culture of the school system.

She enculturated a sense of academic premises, building trusting relationships, validating service rendered by others, and regaining hope for a prosperous future for the young people of the community. Such paramount ideas of working collaboratively together to achieve goals identified and set together as a community were at the forefront of her thinking.

Never for one minute did she think there would be opposition to change. Especially change that proved to be beneficial to the constituents the system served and for the greater good of the community. One would think that a community that knew it needed change and desired change would not obstruct the process of transformation. However, a plentitude of transformational ideas was not enough for the idiosyncrasies of strong-minded political will. Ideas that inspire transformational change that is ruthlessly against opposing strong-minded political will created a barrier.

TEXTBOX 15.1

Create

Ideas that inspire transformational change that is ruthlessly against opposing strong-minded political will sometimes creates a barrier.

Sometimes our own selfishness, perspectives, stereotypes, and truth breed a contemptuous environment. It does not necessarily matter if you provided a recipe for success or a road map to improvement, but it is how well you play the political game. Although the superintendent would strategize and direct the school community through countless pathways to success, the board of education found it more advantageous to stand at the edge of the cliff of destruction until finally falling off the edge.

How could a person see the foreshadowing of the disappointments yet to come? One could not contrive or perceive the obtrusive obstructions that were to come against change and maintaining the status quo. A fault and folly of the superintendent was the failure to engage and stroke the egos of the board of education to their individual personal satisfaction.

Expectations from the community, although this may have been a misinterpretation on the superintendent's part, were to make changes so that their children could have a competitive chance and to be productive. During numerous focus groups, numerous concerns were revealed.

Within the first two months, with the help of staff and a nonprofit organization, focus groups were conducted throughout the city. These groups were composed of parents, students, staff, administrators, nonprofits, business constituents, and representatives from postsecondary institutions. Each group had its various concerns, but there were resounding reoccurring themes that transpired from the focus groups discussions.

These themes were lack of academic rigor and preparation for the workforce, discipline, dropout rate, graduation rate, safety, lack of diversity in the teaching staff, poor inclusion of multiculturalism, and parent engagement. The community's schools were cited by the state as underperforming. Nine out of twenty-two of the district's schools were in academic trouble. The dropout rate exceeded both the state and national rates; students of color were highly identified as having special needs and disciplinary issues. Parents of color felt marginalized, not listened too, and devalued.

Like so many districts, the teaching staff lacked the hue of the students who they were serving. And the growing number of disciplinary issues at the high and middle schools caused increased concern for safety.

But for those in power, the politicians and persons of influence, the expectations were individualized and personalized to meet whatever specific goals met their agenda. Failure had become a platform to lift their political careers; it was a necessity for the community in order to seek additional grant funds and monies for both a failing school system and an impoverished economic community. It was a derogatory label that seemed to open doors to opportunity. A label that some were willing to hold for the benefits it produced.

The superintendent needed to be discerning of the ever-changing needs of the Board's own personal agendas. Superintendents must be politically savvy enough to ascertain the boards' needs which at many times are irrelevant to the efficient functioning of the school system. Some boards are devoted to nepotism, egotism, and cronyism.

Defining her experience in this community as a failure, the superintendent wanted to know where she failed. Where did she go wrong? How could she overcome the obstacles that were ever before her and the possibilities that prevailed on the other side of the battle? Were the odds stacked up against her at the start of the game? Was it caused by someone else or did she cause the failure? Or was there a combination of multiple factors that caused her to sabotage her season of opportunity?

Coming into the game, the playing field was foreign; the superintendent was the first outsider to the district in thirty-five years, the first person of color, and the second female to hold the position. She had to quickly infiltrate foreign soil, set up a house, and amalgamate into a new culture by building relationships without losing self. Cautiously she wanted to show the community her devotion to them by providing evidence of assurances. In her first step, she purchased a house within the city limits. She wanted to show them that she was there to stay.

In one day, a house was found after viewing eleven properties. The realtor was recommended by a board member, who was an ally and now a dear friend. Finally, visiting a development that was on the north end of town, a house was found. It was in a housing development that was only in phase one of the building project; the development's name represented the historical nostalgic heritage of the city.

After viewing three houses in the development that were small and probably better suited for a single person, the superintendent chose a three-bedroom home. She was planning for the future, wanting a family and many parties with staff and the community.

Asking one of the developer's staff to show the model home, she immediately said that this was perfect. Plenty of light emanated through the rooms; a kitchen that could showcase her culinary skills and three bedrooms to provide accommodations to family members as they come to visit. This was a necessity since the town at the time had no hotel and only bed and breakfast establishments.

She purchased a house during a recession and had not sold the one she currently owned in her hometown. This was necessary she felt as a step to assure the community that she was committed and there to stay. Many times she felt this was a foolish mistake, although in her heart she felt that she was there for a lengthy tenure. There really was no guarantee that she would be in the district beyond the contractual commitment. She forgot to assess and consider potentiality or pretenses that this community truly wanted change or not.

As adversity became the fodder for change, as it is the source of many transformations, she quickly moved into protective mode. The house became the sanctuary for peace. No one could penetrate the fortress of safety for her. So the house remained private, not opened to any of her staff. Holding back what little bit of privacy she had and the space that allowed for renewal in order to approach the next day and the next day.

When she realized that she was not comfortable or completely happy in her present circumstance, she quickly began to ask herself three important questions:

Is she right for the work of superintendent?
What can she do differently to make her current tumultuous situation better?
After trying all options, what is the final resolve?

She had trained and worked toward the goal of becoming a superintendent. All of her experiences, training, and education prepared her to do well in this position. Her extensive training in the sciences made her more analytical in her thought process. She scientifically weighed the pros and cons of whether a new idea or strategy was viable and was willing to take risks in strategies that proved to be more effective.

As she dwelled on "being right" for the job, it made her reflect on her purpose in life. Faith-filled individuals have a very different perspective on dealing with life, and decision-making. Spiritually, the superintendent wanted to be in a position to use her gifts and talent in her appointed assignment. Was she positioned in the place where God desired her? Was she within his will and plan for her life? Was she serving as an instrument of his peace?

> **TEXTBOX 15.2**
>
> **Perspective**
>
> The "Right Fit!" Being "right" for the job and being qualified for the job could be construed differently. Is there an underlying meaning to the "right fit?" Use multiple perspectives or lens to reflect on this question.

Could she truly make an impact that was for the good of the community? Intellectually, she began to doubt her preparedness for the position even though her knowledge, training, education, and experiences said otherwise. Egocentric, this was the highest point of her career that she could achieve! She defined this as success, and to fail at this position would have nullified all the positive impacts made along the career pathway. It is remarkable how one significant event in your life can shape the future and dismiss any good done in the past.

Superintendence was the top of her field, nowhere else to go! She had arrived at her destination eager, willing, optimistic, idealistic, visionary, and hopeful. Her optimistic view of the world made her think that she would have support because "we all want the same goal and that is for the children of the community to really achieve their potential." How did she forget about the empowered versus those who are powerless?

Inane was she to think for a moment that within an institution, those who reign actually care about the well-being of their subjects. That in this world, politics rules, and the personal agendas of those in control stronghold the less empowered. And the less empowered remain powerless and dependent upon those in power. This further gives those in power, yet more power. Along with this power come purpose, control, wealth, and meaning. It is cyclic in nature, an unending cycle.

Quickly, the superintendent learned the streets and neighborhoods, the cultural groups that made up north, south, and west ends of this port city. For the east was the sea. She attended events not just to be visible but to gain an understanding of the mores, traditions, and habits of her neighbors.

She read, studied, ate cultural dishes, and asked questions about the history and heritage of the people and the city. Tapping into this information, the superintendent enriched programs by including diverse cultural groups. This garnered a sense of pride in the school system.

Building relationships with support groups, outreaching to resources in surrounding suburbia, and fostering personal friendships, the superintendent continued to gain insight about the opposition that she was up against. In some ways, she tried to balance her work life by maintaining personal hobbies but her position became her life; this was evident by the devotion of time given and the constant twenty-four-hour thought process of "what can we do better" to improve the schools. Pen and paper are always on the nightstand.

Her expectations were high! She wanted change for the school system; not to glorify self but to provide opportunities for thousands of individuals similar to the opportunities afforded to her. Overall she believed this was her calling and purpose in life for this appointed time. To her, children were the most important asset to a community. They should be highly invested in producing a yield that gives insurmountable gains whether to the local community or to society as a whole. If she had an ulterior motive, then like all humans, it was to be needed by another.

Her intentions were true and genuine. Did she lose sight or focus of the goals? No, she was there for the specific purpose of changing the way the school system performed, which required progressive forward thinking. New goals and progressive action did not corroborate with the direct wishes of the powerful political elite that had survived decades and controlled many facets of the municipal departments.

Would she like to blame her lack of success for not completing her tenure with someone else? Yes! However, she must take joint responsibility for what went wrong and what went right in her two-year stead of the most difficult test of her life thus far. She was sure there will be more tests in life, for this last one did not kill her, although it came very close. However, it has become a reminder of humility and a point of reflection.

SECTION 2: FALLING SHORT OF THE RIGHT FIT

Triumphant entry into the city was full of joy, excitement, and great expectation of change. And so she was deemed as a sort of savior for the people and children; here is someone who spoke of change, had a plan, and believed in executing the plan. As the media implicated, she was the "right fit."

People have a tendency to place leaders on pedestals with the expectation to carry out change that in most cases is grandiose, meeting the vision which they have encapsulated in their mind. For some, such change is revolutionary, almost pinnacle to what our nation is facing today with civil dissonance.

Yet, they are also sharply critical of leaders when they do not comply with their objectives.

The superintendent did not realize the type of change truly expected of her, which was to only help change the regime of power and not actually make changes that directly impacted the people's lives for the betterment of their community and future. So for those at the helm of the regime, she had fallen short of their expectations. How fickle is the human emotion!

Her first obstacle was to lead change in a community divided by status quo versus the desired improvement. She was caught in a trench. Two polar sides vying for what they viewed as important. One side wanted power and control; change was okay if they could wield it. The other side wanted the schools to do better for their children. Children exited the system with a sub-par education. Statistics were clear; this was a system that was failing some of its children. Second, the dysfunctional relationship with the board became an impeding roadblock that had to constantly be navigated.

Some of the nets that held the system back from progressive improvements directly affected the quality of education offered to the community's children. Third, obstacle was the economic climate of the community. The school system was valued as being the primary employer of the city. Very little industry and few jobs were available but the community was ripe with nonprofits. Movement to focus on green sustainable energy provided some newer thinking jobs and opportunities in the community. But this was limited.

Students who completed their postsecondary schooling had very little to look forward to in the job market if they returned to the community. This was a broken cistern that was dried out; the community was preparing students for what they saw as an unpromising future. With very few prospects of jobs, some students became hopeless or considered no rationale to succeed.

On the bright side, students who were not afraid or netted into the community could venture outside and find a wealth of opportunities. Those invested in their community would remain or give back, but most of those who sought better lives would not return.

The system was closed off to outside leadership for thirty-five years, and being the first person of color and a female, she found many challenges occurred because of the very nature of her being and not her skills. This was a fourth obstacle dealing with cultural, generational, and gender differences.

It was clear that the board wanted a person that they could micro-manage and keep the status quo. Even though she clearly shared with the school board her vision for the district within the strategic plan, it became clear that her thinking was too progressive for this district, and the push to move forward was hard and strenuous.

No matter how often she tried to extend the olive branch to the board, it did not matter. Efforts continued only on her part and the board had its own agenda. She could not compromise her belief in giving the best to children, and at times this came with sacrifices. There was much time devoted to improving the academic rigor and professionalism of staff, working with families, working with community partners, and postsecondary institutions. However, this fell short when it came to saving face with some of the members of the board.

In reflecting, the superintendent began to assess the emotional roller coaster of feelings that were immersed into regret, depression, fear, anger, and defeat. All she wanted was to be invisible. Yet when emotionally broken, faith helps us meet God at the well for strength and perseverance. Those without a spiritual connection become broken and never truly heal.

The superintendent had withdrawn herself from the world and became very selective with whom she interacted with, limiting conversations and using single sentence responses like, "I'm okay." This was more to reassure herself that she was truly alright!

She felt a need to do this in order to heal without bitterness, to strengthen her broken spirit, to reflect on the decisions and choices made, and how could she have better avoided the land mines that were intently laid for her destruction. She reflected on how she could have better played the political game. She prayed to God to restore her and remove from her any memory of this place.

This story of the superintendent's journey shows what could happen as a result of broken relationships and lack of trust. As a response, the superintendent avoided people. More specifically, she avoided the board members and associated politicians. She would register and signup for every professional developmental workshop, conference, or seminar, just not to be available. She kept her accessibility to a minimum, avoiding any unnecessary interactions.

She began to document and record conversations, collecting transcripts that may be used to support her stance or protect her from criticism. "To avoid people, she would walk miles passing local watering holes to draw water at the hottest periods of the day." She found safe havens, and there she would linger or hide.

In those safe havens, she would visit school buildings, spending time with administrators and staff, those who she trusted and were loyal to the mission and goals of the district. Not necessarily loyal to her. She protected herself to avoid people's judgmental stares and negative conversations that pointed back to failures. Such conversations would linger with statements such as "You should know your limitations; this is a tough place to navigate!" "This is a unique place that does not take kindly to outsiders."

She had imposed self-barriers and inherited system-imposed barriers. She perceived nonacceptance of her because of her ethnicity and gender as an African American female and very little trust because of it. These system-imposed barriers included the denied reality of the need for change, nostalgic traditionalism, closed-off system, and political depravity. All these barriers were hard factual realities that she had to press her way through.

A second response to the obstacles at hand was to throw herself into her work. One has a tendency to overcompensate to prove self-worth and value when there is a lack of trust. Nonacceptance of her ability and skills that she brought to the table was now in the background of the strife between the board and herself.

Reflecting on the successes that came out of this experience, at the time, the district had nine schools identified in need of improvement. Working with staff, administration, and consultants, four schools were removed from the list. Attention was on rethinking authentic literacy and numeracy and differentiating instruction to meet the needs of the students in the classroom. The following changes had to be made in the district and became the foci:

- The way they thought about literacy
- Building vocabulary, syntax, voice, and text connection through writing and oral communication
- Redirecting the work of instructional coaches
- Increasing teacher and student expectation
- Goal setting for each student and flexible grouping
- Instructional strategies that included guided reading
- Coteaching strategies to assist students with special needs
- Assessment benchmarks to measure progress
- Incorporate instructional strategies that assist diverse learners
- Increase rigor and expectation, more problem-solving
- Provide supplemental support for students
- Provide opportunity for students who are ready to take higher-level courses

Actions were intentional; the strategic plan became a living document. Goals and strategies were put into action with accountability. Decision-making and branding were aligned with the strategic plan. Constantly keeping goals and mission in the forefront, every document, social media post, speech, and message included the district's focus! Central office staff joined in the accountable talk and the majority of school leadership came on board with the understanding of what improvement meant in terms of measurable results.

TPQ

1) As a leader, how do you view failure as an opportunity for growth in leadership? How do you gauge when it is time to let go?

2) What perceivable traits of leadership and personality identify with the phrase "right fit"? How can these same traits be a detriment or an advantage to a leader's success in a district?

CHAPTER KEY IDEAS

1. Experiential testimony of a first superintendence in the midst of nets, trenches, sinkholes, and cisterns serves as a sage to prepare others who desire this role.
2. When confronting obstacles in both leadership and the educational system, one must be resilient.

Chapter 16

What Do We Say?

> The ultimate measure of a man is not where he stands in moments of comfort and convenience, but where he stands at times of challenge and controversy.
>
> —Martin Luther King Jr.

What perspective does one take when the reference point of life becomes the circumstance that you are living? It inverts the view of life. It becomes a net and forms a dividing trench. Warren Bennis and Robert Thomas wrote an article in the *Harvard Business Review* that described crucible experiences that shape or transform leaders' character traits. They defined a crucible as a "transformative experience through which an individual comes to a new or an altered sense of identity" (Bennis and Thomas 2002, 4).

If the superintendent in the vignette of chapter 15 was to look at her crucible experience of her first superintendence, she would categorically describe it as adverse. Adversity reveals a great deal about one's true identity and ability to relate to others. Within the experience, superficiality of "wanting change" and "actually wanting change" was two very different realities. Such that she was sought out to be an instrument of change, but the true reality was only to change the face that was in the position prior.

True reality is vividly exposed when innovative change begins to occur. Those who mock and are naysayers raise their fierce talons; the face of jealousy to popularity and an alternate way of thinking ensues. Jealousy comes with the charge of innovation. Power struggles often bring jealousy, envy, and strife within the strata of hierarchy. This became the case when the superintendent began to progressively move forward with systemic changes.

> **TEXTBOX 16.1**
>
> Power struggles within relationships often bring jealousy, envy, and strife.

Such simplicity of doing what was right was questioned as to why the previous administration could not move the needle of improvement. Haunted by the previous administration, it became a test of bravado, as a colleague in the same ranks was used to pivot his loyalty and allegiance to the district and community against a newcomer. The former superintendent was still working behind the scenes orchestrating chaos and confusion to cause division.

A dangerous destructive net that really did not make sense, until the superintendent realized that there was a camp that did not want her to be successful. Why? Her presence represented a whole new brand for the district—young, African American, female, from outside of the district, and from outside of the state. She was a nuance, she was different.

This was the true reality of change desired by the district, not improving the academic performance of students, closing achievement gaps, and accountability of staff. Her face represented the district or a new way of thinking about the district.

Branding messages impart the vision of what an organization is about. The superintendent's very nature represented a different statement about the district. She was new, innovative, diverse, female, academically and intellectually focused. Polar opposite to the former leadership, the previous superintendent was a veteran educator, loyal to the district, male, and a traditionalist. He was politically connected, knew the right connections, and had many familial relations in the system.

Crucibles force one to confront the distorted picture of oneself that the circumstance creates. No doubt producing an overwhelming flood of emotional feelings puts one in defense mode, anger, defeat, and even withdrawal. Polar to these emotions, the circumstance made the superintendent press even harder to make sure her P's and Q's were extraordinarily checked.

> **TEXTBOX 16.2**
>
> Crucibles force one to confront the distorted picture of oneself that the circumstance creates. Otherwise, it becomes a net that traps and impacts the success of the partnership.

Making sure that her decisions, actions, and practices were integral in alignment with both vision and mission, such drive made the naysayers even angrier. But, if one does not confront, then it can become a net that traps and impacts the partnership that is necessary for the vision and mission moving forward.

It became crystal clear to her one day, instead of putting a plate of cookies out for the committee's consumption, she decided to serve. One committee member remarked, "Now see, that is nice." Knowing her place! One of servitude! She really had to come to grips with this because although the person meant it as an attack on her ethnicity and social inferiority, she had to reprogram her mind to think about servitude as a strong characteristic of an effective leader. Not servitude in view of slavery.

Leaders must lead out of eagerness to serve not of obligation or fear. Later, this same person would call her to task about not being a sufficient role model for young African American girls. You cannot imagine how this statement cut the superintendent to the core of her identity. It knocked the breath out of her lungs as she grasped for a soft complacent response to this critique of her character.

In her mind, the following monologue occurred, "What do you mean I am not a role model to African American girls? I have the highest position in this educational system that a person could attain. I have degrees and certifications. Modeling the mantra, you too can do it. I have been an advocate for and mentor to many. I even concerned myself around social issues of sex trafficking, domestic violence, and teenage pregnancy that are primarily affecting our students."

Wow! In response to this, she became hypersensitive and didn't know if she should begin to rock natural hair and wear a dashiki to the next board meeting in order to meet the expectation, stereotypes and platitudes of her bosses. Regardless, her lesson here was to lead by example and not by force. Her tongue gave apologetic words for not meeting this expectation. Oh what grace!

Amazingly, adversity makes you realize your insufficiencies, such areas that need to be developed or stretched. Frustrations come and can paralyze you if you are not sure who you are as a person.

The superintendent's identity was being defined by outward and not internal characteristics and by people who were not interested in the internal depth of the person. Such limits of defining only by outward characteristics allow others to interject stereotypes or learned perceptions of how those with such physical characteristics are "to be." This makes it difficult to build trust, especially when one is not complying with the stereotype.

Such relationships are pretentious and substantially short term; divorce is eminent. There will always be suspicion that you are going beyond boundaries which one has placed upon you.

A lesson of adversity and perseverance is that in the midst of stressful nets, we are to continue to express joy! The superintendent continued to smile although internally her spirit was addressing rejection, devaluation, and inferiority. In her upbringing, she was taught that faith is refined by fire. Crucibles are furnaces of affliction that require us to trust God for the outcome. This was a time she was trusting in him like never before. Definitely, impurities were falling off of her. Better than a sinking feeling of the ground collapsing underneath her.

We cannot bear the weight of not knowing self and at the same time help others (students) who are coming into purpose. It is contradictory. Controlling the emotions when disrupters of your peace throw darts is essential. We must learn to face our giants with the perspective of overcoming and not fearing. Knowing that you have been appointed to a position for such a time is truly a faith walk. It changes the perspective and increases the courage to continue in the position, enabling you to maintain strenuous work without the affirmation of your abilities.

Some relationships are not meant to be healed and in this case the healing came within her. As she forgave the difficulties, the people, and the place, she forged on to her next superintendence. Effective leaders are always in transformation; they never stagnate. This comes through the lessons and reflections from the crucibles that come our way. Important to note are the transformational changes, this is what better prepares you for the next phase of life.

TEXTBOX 16.3

Effective leaders are always in some state of transformation; they never stagnate.

As for the nets, trenches, cisterns, and sinkholes, we can be held back from doing good work, or progressively forge ahead to change. Some nets we create ourselves and are not always outside agents trying to capture, while other nets are intentional, withholding us from progressing.

A quality of "good" leaders is that when failure occurs they take responsibility. In the sense of this failed opportunity and relationship, the superintendent decided to resign. Some may say she was pushed out, but we always have choices. The experience could have captured her and held her back from ever trying this position again, but it did not.

And although difficult, the trench caused by broken relationships is very paralyzing and is also polarizing. In this case, the relationship between the superintendent and the board of education became an unhealable covenant. Division brings a great deal of strife and if both parties are not willing to heal the divide, it is impossible. Trenches are narrow, as is some of our thinking about others. We have a tendency to categorize people, it's cultural. It helps us to perceive if it is someone we want to trust.

Trust becomes difficult when there are so many barriers built from the foundation of fear that prevents a successful relationship. One does not have to yield power to gain trust, but one must believe they can trust. There must be assurance; it cannot be a pending sinkhole and contracts are not enough of a guarantee. Trust must be communicated in actions, words, and deeds.

Sustaining relationships comes with communication that is a two-way process. Communication is a word that can be so easily manipulated to describe secure ground or poor footing. In one moment, the solid ground underneath your feet could become a gaping sinkhole if you failed to give the desired information. How well one communicates depends upon what the receiver of the communication feels is acceptable. You could be perfect intel and be labeled a poor communicator if the information was not appealing to the receiver.

Experiences can strengthen or break us; they can make us more compassionate toward others or bitter. Such parallel reactions to difficult crucibles could captivate us in cisterns designated as prisons. Time is said to heal difficult trials. Separation from trials may eliminate the drudgery but memory holds such difficult experiences in our hippocampus.

Similar experiences trigger remembrance of these experiences. This could hold us captive too if we fail to properly heal from difficulty. But if we grow from our difficulty, how much stronger are we when the next trial comes? We know that we are healed by our response in similar environments.

Complexity of systems intertwined with relationships truly challenges us during any change process. If we want to reform the educational system, truly reform, then it is time to reflect on the brokenness of our relationships at each strata level of the educational system and address the political tenor and divisiveness. These are the primary causes of making reform efforts too difficult to sustain.

TPQ

1) What strategies do you employ to overcome obstacles? What could the superintendent in the vignette have done differently to prevent the experience? What could she do differently to restore the relationship?
2) Think about your self-worth. What opinions and values have you placed on yourself? Draft a personal profile.

3) Describe a transformative experience in your career. How has this past experience altered your sense of identity? Were there any distortions that affected your self-worth?

CHAPTER KEY IDEAS

1. Adversity in life makes one realize their insufficiencies and areas that need development. But, if we grow from our difficulties, we will be stronger for the next trial.
2. It is difficult to build trusting relationships when others project stereotypes or learned perceptions onto your identity.

Part 8

DISTRICTS' RESPONSE TO ADDRESSING NETS, TRENCHES, SINKHOLES, AND CISTERNS

Chapter 17

District 1—Interweaving Coalitions and Strengthening the Mesh

> Vision without action is merely a dream. Action without vision just passes the time. Vision with action can change the world.
> —Joel A. Barker

Each of the three districts addressed the obstacles imagined as nets, trenches, sinkholes, and cisterns discussed in earlier chapters in different ways. Many of the strategies the districts employed were intentional with expected outcomes. Some of the strategies were circumstantial in that it was a forced change, while in other cases, it was a result of taking advantage of the opportunity to change.

District 1's net was visible in the achievement gaps among their student population. Focusing on the changing needs of the student population, district 1 seriously considered the importance of addressing cultural differences and stereotypes believed to prohibit or limit student engagement and the motivation to learn. Their strategy was to implement the research and practices of cultural proficiency by renewing their pedagogical practices, curriculum, assessment, and policies. The target content area was literacy. In doing this, the hope was to alleviate the ever-widening achievement gaps in various student subgroups.

These student subgroups consisted primarily of students of color, special needs, and impoverished. Because of the prevailing cultural differences and stereotypes against members of these subgroups, it impacted teachers' beliefs and expectations about students' academic performance. This district saw hope in targeting factors that impeded students' engagement, comfortability and motivation to learn, school attendance, and a sense of belonging as important factors to addressing the barriers preventing students' academic success.

In the last decade of the twentieth century, district 1 was recognized as a rigorous, prestigious district. Fast forward to 2021, test scores have seen small incremental declines in English Language Arts and small incremental increases in mathematics. Gaps among student groups remain. The largest gaps were between white and African American students and white and special education students (see table 17.1).

What has changed in the district? There was a demographic shift in the student population. The student population is currently 5,344 students. Forty-four percent of the students are from low-income families, 60.4 percent students are of color, 19 percent have special needs, and 5.7 percent are English language learners. To address the needs of an increasing number of low-income families, special needs, and English language learners, state funding intervened to support the district at the expense of rigorous course work.

Downward cycle of academic performance qualified the district for additional state funding to address the achievement gap. The district framed the net by focusing on five essential elements driven by courageous conversations (Singleton 2006, 2014) around race where differences were assessed, labeled, framed, and adaptations to differences resulting in an organizational culture change. From this, an assessment of practices, policies, and procedures categorized the competency level and gauged where the district was in reaching equity for all its constituents.

The district acknowledged the changing demographics and recognized that how they viewed the change and treated those causing the change would significantly impact the direction the district needed to steer. Ignoring the increasing diversity or treating it as a challenge would only demonstrate intolerance, a devaluing, and or even blindness to the need. Such action further creates dissonance and greater conflict.

Opposite to this sentiment was to be responsive to the increasing diversity and see it as strength. Systemwide adaptations and continuous improvement

Table 17.1 District Average in Percent of Students' Performance at or above Proficiency on SBAC (Smarter Balanced Assessment Consortium) in English Language Arts (ELA) and Mathematics during 2015 and 2019, the Last Scores prior to the Pandemic

	District 1 Student SBAC Scores 2015 versus 2019			
Student	ELA 2015	Math 2015	ELA 2019	Math 2019
All	67.8	58.1	64.9	61.8
African American	58.0	46.5	55.6	51.1
Hispanic	61.8	51.8	59.3	56.1
White	75.0	65.9	73.8	71.2
Special Education	49.0	40.0	45.9	41.9

Source: EdSight data portal.

required change in district's policies on attendance, discipline, and identification of students for special education. Instructional practices were broadened to be culturally responsive and more supports were integrated into the classroom to target intervention strategies.

> **TEXTBOX 17.1**
>
> **Changing Practice for Equity**
>
> 1) Assessment of cultural knowledge
> 2) Valuing diversity
> 3) Addressing conflict
> 4) Adaptation to differences
> 5) Integration of cultural knowledge
>
> Five points adapted from R. Lindsey, L. Roberts, and F. Campbelljones; Five Essential Elements as Leverage Points for Change in the Culturally Proficient School (2013, 82).

Cultural responsiveness or proficiency is an effective way to address cultural differences that impact or influence what and how students learn (Lindsey, Roberts, and Campbelljones 2013; Lindsey et al. 2018). District 1 wanted to target the changing diversity and address the emerging cultures by acknowledging the benefits of incorporating these differences with intentionality to create a better environment and by motivating and engaging students in the learning process.

It was the belief of the leadership that the teaching staff and community's indifference to the diverse cultural groups, that it was now serving, created low expectations for students' ability to learn. For the district, both ethnicity and social-economic status were the dividing factors of the indifference.

Supporters of cultural proficiency have devised a continuum that reflects the various cultural responses to cultural differences. Points on the continuum consist of cultural destructiveness, cultural incapacity, cultural blindness, cultural precompetence, cultural competence, and cultural proficiency. Extremities of this continuum show the disparaging nature of what poor cultural relationships could develop if an organization is not continuously moving to improve in response to the needs of their community.

Staff within the district were all over the continuum which reflected in their expectation toward students' academic performance. Addressing the various points on the continuum, collaborative efforts went into developing the staff's cultural proficiency by establishing outside partnerships with agencies that could assist the district in changing the culture.

Professional development ensued with the partnering work of NUA focusing on differentiated instructional practices specifically in literacy, alternative forms of assessment, student voice, choice, and rigor. Rolling this out throughout prekindergarten to grade 12 was to affect one's knowledge of diverse cultures and differences and to expand the resources available to build respectful relationships among cultural groups.

Working partnership with National Urban Alliance assisted the district in focusing on the widening gaps in the reading achievement of their students. Students identified as not reading on grade level received intensive intervention as part of regular instruction that significantly accelerated their academic progress. Literature used for instruction included works and interests of other cultures, not limiting to the dominant culture only but yielding multicultural diversity.

Also, the use of heuristics assisted with executive functioning and study strategies. Assessment was used to monitor student progress and achievement of district goals. Northwest Evaluation Association (NWEA) testing system, an adaptive approach to tracking student academic progress and growth, was the diagnostic of choice. A clear road map to the expected outcomes was strategically planned by the district. Utilized student choice for classroom assessments and preference for demonstrating understanding.

Parent programs such as literacy, math, and science nights served as means to educate parents about the curriculum standards and how parents can continue to teach at home with simple support strategies.

Addressing equity across the district and what equity actually means in the dynamics of the district were critical in moving toward improvement. Some of the tactics included working with the union to reassign staff throughout the district, allowing teachers to be the lead in the change, and introducing alternative programs for students to earn credit toward their diploma. A thread is interwoven throughout by knitting together the different initiatives and showing how each initiative contributed to the final goal of the district. That final goal was improving academic success for all students and closing the achievement gaps.

Socioeconomic pressures, disparity, and inequity were very prevalent at the elementary level because of the number of elementary schools throughout the town. Parents, community members, and staff always questioned inequities. However, the district resolved many of these issues in the upper grades by the one middle and one high school, better addressing the have and have nots, the demands from the educated families versus under-educated families.

Trusting relationships at the various tiers of the hierarchy were visible in the district. Both board and administration understood the importance of partnering with the community and outside partnership to drive improvement and sustain best practices. Intentionally not trying to pit one against the other, the board and superintendent tried to create an environment of trust and transparency, preventing the digging of the trench.

As the years passed in the district and leadership changed at the various tiers of the hierarchy, many of these innovative practices and partnerships were not sustained. New vision and goals came with a new superintendent and changing school board. Societal and cultural shifts created a different direction to achieving improvement. Funding changed and was redirected to meet new initiatives. Although the gaps still remained and questions of equity prevalent in the minds of parents and the community, the approach to the focus changed.

This is what happens when a strong foundation is not present or preserved and new foci cover the old, until layers and layers of new initiatives weigh down the infrastructure. The district's academic performance was stagnated and hidden by data points.

Board of education relationship with the superintendent was viable; however, there was a fixed mindset of how students of color, disabilities, and low-income status learn and their capacity to achieve. Although rich standards are prescribed at each grade level, mindsets had become the snare to what actually manifested in the classroom by the way it is taught, what is taught, depths of what is taught, and how it is assessed. Measuring student ability, the rigor of instruction and curriculum, and the teacher's expectation of the student were driven by the entrenched mindset that defined students' capacity.

TPQ

1) Academic achievement gaps have persisted in our nation's history since the onset of public schooling. How would you approach closing such gaps?

CHAPTER KEY IDEAS

1. Responses to the obstacles leaders have to contend with will vary based upon the needs, politics, and culture of the community they serve.
2. Some strategies to address obstacles that confront leaders are: to become more culturally responsive to diversity in communities, build partnerships with organizations that can help facilitate change, use assessment to monitor student growth and diagnostically identify target areas to assist

students, educating the whole family and seeing parents as an extension of the classroom, and employing an equity model in all aspects of decision-making.

Chapter 18

District 2—Embattlement of the Casted Net

Everyone designs who devises courses of action aimed at changing existing situations into preferred ones.

—Herbert A. Simon

An embattlement of notorious casting out of the net, District 2 was in an ever-looming weave of mediocrity and low achievement. A once booming and rich economy, the city housing the district like so many municipalities failed to revitalize itself and find a new niche for economic growth and development.

Unlike the revitalization projects of Cincinnati, Milwaukee, and Minneapolis, these are all manufacturing cities that have successfully undergone reurbanization. This city was struggling to find its new niche. On the economic decline, it impacted the schools, or some in the community say vice versa. There is definitely a codependent relationship that determines the success of the two. But the focus during this period of time was, "How to regain the city's footing?" The approach to reurbanization focused on the historical, regional, political connection, and demographic makeup of the city.

Growth and economic development are key to reenergizing cities and communities. When cities create conditions that embrace the diversity of their residents and the inclusion of households of all incomes across all neighborhoods, revitalization is evident. We see this in the cities listed earlier. District 2's city leaders understood this and had the foresight of collaborating with different groups, using the arts, culture, and historical heritage to catapult the city into the twenty-first century.

The municipality's revitalization plan included partnerships with the school district along with businesses and organizations for change. Performing and visual arts was the heartbeat of the city. Finest symphony orchestra, Broadway ready theatrical productions, and bohemian art studios layered the streets of downtown, drawing many residents from surrounding towns.

But the significant problem was the development of new industries to bring high-paying and high-skilled jobs to the city. Technology went green with a focus on the environment. Companies with this kind of vision were drawn to the industrial park and the school district along with postsecondary institutions began to change their curriculum and course offerings to attract and prepare the type of student needed for these futuristic jobs.

This was all the seeds of urban revitalization, but nostalgia and tradition became obstacles to new ideas, power struggles, positions, and control prevented or showed change. Because of the division and divisiveness with power structure, good ideas from opposite poles began to push against each other and thus the formation of a trench.

Power struggles resulted, creating polarizing groups and divisiveness. Many of these groups were based on cultural lines causing isolation of other groups. Leadership was charged to work around the barriers and tried to bring key power players together for change. The community expressed change, but it was difficult to move the needle. Even with the infrastructure and urban revitalization, new zoning separated neighborhoods from the city center.

Affordable housing pushed inclusionary zoning, and the reconstruction of the waterway began to open up those neighborhoods that were isolated. At large the city was closed off to other communities and so was the school district. It was closed off, cloistered, and fixed in its practices.

Strategic planning was the leadership's tool and fore thinking of bringing the divided community together to create the driving force that would guide and direct the necessary change. As a collaborative team, administration, teachers, parents, board of education, and community members held community conversations throughout the different neighborhoods. At each neighborhood meeting, the group met as a whole for the explanation and intent of the meeting and how information was to be gathered and used to set goals for the district.

The whole group was then divided into smaller intimate groups where team members lead the conversation and a second team member recorded the information. The group reconvened at the end of the session for a reporting out. These types of sessions were repeated throughout the city including a separate session for businesses and nonprofits and for secondary institution representatives were also conducted.

During these conversations, a set number of questions drove the discussion; a team member recorded the information on flip charts and posted the information during the discussion. The questions were as follows:

1. What do you think needs to happen in the public schools so that schools are friendly and welcoming places for parents, caretakers, and community members?
   a. Think about the type of experiences you have had and the type of experiences you would want to have as you walk in to the city schools? What does the school system need to do to make this happen?
2. What do you think successful school education should be like?
   a. What types of programs and classes should be offered?
   b. What should students learn? What should be happening in the classrooms, how should teachers teach?
   c. What types of programs, coursework, or learning can we add to make the schools more appealing, interesting, and responsive to the needs of our students?
   d. What types of relationships should occur at the school level between students, parents, and the community?
3. What do you think we should do to increase the academic success of students and ensure that students are promoted and ready to become successful and contributing citizens in society?
   a. Please share with us the types of academic support activities that we should have in place for all students. You may want to include teaching methods, resources, and other suggestions.
      i. What should we do at the elementary level?
      ii. What should we do at the middle school level?
      iii. What should we do at the high school level?
      iv. What should we do to prepare students for postsecondary education?
4. How would you suggest the schools work with students who are having difficulty, exhibiting behavioral issues (poor attendance, tardiness, bullying, not following rules, swearing, and talking back to teachers)?

Questions were slightly modified for business/nonprofit organizations to include:

What do you think we should do to increase the academic success of high-school students and ensure that students are ready for postsecondary learning or employment in this area? Identify the necessary skills for readiness.

Recorded information from all the groups was analyzed for common reoccurring themes. For example, one of the concerns that surfaced in the discussion was the inequity in funding. In turn, these themes identified the mission, vision, and priorities of the guiding principles for decision-making and four main goals, as discussed below.

From the community conversations, the mindset within the district was refreshed. All decision-making became student-centered, and the underlying belief was that all children have the right to achieve their potential and can succeed academically. School culture and climate must be responsive to the diverse needs of the students. These were the guiding principles to help formulate a cohesive strategy of practice in the policies, curriculum and pedagogy, decision-making, and budgeting. Effectually, four goals were established:

1. Set high academic standards for all students and believe they can achieve them.
2. Create a positive school culture that builds character and self-confidence.
3. Engage parents and community in the learning process.
4. Establish a professional staff that demonstrates quality, diversity, and a strong background in content knowledge and pedagogy.

Deep within the strategic plan objectives, actions, roles of responsible parties, expected outcomes, and timeline spelled out the intentional strategies to obtain these goals. The plan was a result and reflection of listening to community voices and threading desires, concerns, expectations, and issues of equity together.

This viable document began to move the thresholds that the net had caused by the provision of increased opportunities for students to learn, responsiveness to cultural differences in a positive manner, increased partnerships that benefited students and teachers, a renewed hope for the system in producing and providing the type of education the community desired. These goals help the district to focus on the day-to-day work and connection and meaning to the work at hand. Partners and employees began to feel valued and true contributors to the work.

Changes provided increased opportunities for students to accelerate their learning through revisions of the curriculum and course offerings, review of the magnet school programs, and parents' options of choice within the district. Coherent curricular focus across academic content areas improved the cultural responsiveness and rigor.

Likewise, the review of the arts and expansion of world language programs as important components to student learning and the incorporation of the town's history and unique diversity within the social studies program increased the relevancy and student engagement. Partnerships with postsecondary institutions and local organizations that focused on marine life science provided additional resources and opportunities for students.

Dynamics of relationships and the trenches that caused separations was the main obstacle holding this district back from any sustainable change and reform. What was divulged during the community conversations was nothing unique from the many issues most urban districts find. Parents felt their voices were not being heard, especially parents of color, and lack of appreciation for the different cultures that made up the community.

Heavily steeped in this district's culture was a fear of retribution. It was a fear-based work culture. Fear being the motivator negatively affected work performance, psychological well-being, and relationships. This was a result of former practices that employed scare tactics to control the behavior of employees. The outcome was resentful compliance and it affected both staff and students' performance. Part of the strategy was to change this culture with the infusion of coaching, mentoring, delegating, and transparency, all opposites to micromanaging and one-way communication.

Relationships between the superintendent and board of education were strained, two factions of principals formed one giving their allegiance to the old guard, and the second embracing the new. Those of the old guard hiding their ineffectiveness with the entitlement of position based upon relation to the former leadership.

Teacher and superintendent relationships were fortified but tested. It was new to trust someone who was true to their word and took action for the major good and not individual gain. Teachers were in survival mode and afraid to talk to their principal or the superintendent. It was a culture that turned colleagues into competitors rather than collaborators. All of these relational barriers had an effect on students and negatively branded the reputation of the district.

Help came from the community partnerships through rebranding and speaking of the positive things that can come from the school district. But, the culture of retribution was deep and difficult to etch away.

Within the district plan, both short-term and long-term objectives with predicted outcomes and metrics were relevant to the needs of the district and the desires of the community. Although an intentional plan that provided the necessary context for improvement within the frameworks of three years, it was thwarted by the trenches that formed and the leadership not being able to see the plan completely through to its end.

TPQ

1) What are the impacts on school districts and their role in revitalization and economic development within their community? How can school districts help their community find new glory? What are the unique challenges of small rural districts versus urban districts?

CHAPTER KEY IDEAS

1. There is a codependent relationship between a municipality or community's economic development and its school district performance. Vitality occurs when diversity is embraced.
2. Strategic planning is a necessary process for change but is only successful with implementation, actionable measures, revisions, checks, and balances. It is meant to purposefully guide and direct change within the organization, both logically and systematically.
3. Strategic planning empowers all stakeholders within the organization to contribute to the change process by opening up dialogue and communication.

Chapter 19

District 3—Building the Framework for a Strong Foundation

> A Successful man is one who can lay a firm foundation with bricks others have thrown at him.
>
> —David Brinkley

Like District 2, District 3 was also trapped in a cycle of mediocrity and failure but wanted an exit ramp to a road of success. Realizing that the students' needs have changed, students were attending school with social and emotional baggage. But this did not warrant an excuse for academic failure. Yes, students' needs have changed, but what changes have been made to address those needs?

District 3's achievement gap among their student population was socioeconomic. At the time, 50 percent of students received free or subsidized lunch. Many of the families had Department of Children and Families Services involved in their lives and grandparents were serving as custodial parents. This was a demographic change for the district within the past ten years. It was also next door to a refuge city causing the English learner and immigrant population to grow. The diversity and needs of their students were changing as their struggle to show academic improvement on state measures increased.

District 3 approached the obstacles by addressing the social and emotional aspects of children's needs. Although not labeled at the time, it was a multitiered system of supports (MTSS) that addressed the social-emotional learning from prekindergarten through twelfth grade. It was the belief of the district that until these needs were met, it was difficult to address academic learning.

Using an integrated multitiered system of support, the district incorporated strategies for regulating behavior at the elementary and middle-school level with the implementation of mindfulness strategies, PBIS, DARE program, executive functioning, and other responsive classroom practices to bring about educational equity and excellence. At the high school level, implemented strategies focused on college and career readiness and continuation of executive function skills, capstone projects, and service-learning projects.

TEXTBOX 19.1 MULTITIERED SYSTEM OF SUPPORTS

Level of Support	Support Strategies	
Deeper Treatment Intervention Strategies	Third-Party Counseling Resource Therapeutic Placement Safe Spaces Alternative Programs Modified School Day Small Group Counseling	Behavior Specialist Sensory Walls Credit Recovery Check-ins One-on-One Counseling
Prevention Strategies	Mindfulness Activities PBIS DARE Responsive Classroom Restorative Discipline Executive Functioning School-Based Health Clinic	Student Success Plans Capstone Projects Service Projects

Teachers implemented practices within their classrooms that created safe spaces for students to share. This changed the climate and set the tone of the school. Elementary schools were the strongest to approach the needs and had strong teams of support consisting of social worker, school psychologist, regular and special education teacher, principal, and as needed a behavioral specialist to work with students who were exhibiting malign behaviors or reacting to life stressors or trauma. This team effort went beyond the classroom at times working with the entire family.

Additionally, the district partnered with a community-based health organization to provide three school-based clinics. These clinics were strategically placed in the neighborhoods where children were at the most risk and impoverished. At the middle and high school, clinics included a mental health component.

Curricular changes and practices at all levels embedded best strategies to help students build self and social awareness, regulation of emotions and behavior, goal setting and decision-making. All students at each level were required to set goals within their success plan that were to follow them throughout the grades. Goals were set for academic development, social-emotional and physical wellness, and career development.

District 3—Building the Framework for a Strong Foundation

Teachers differentiated instruction based upon the needs of their students. Strategically, they focused on literacy/English Language Arts and mathematics, and at the secondary level the focus was on college and career readiness.

Both the culture and dynamics of the town lead to high proclivity rates of mental illness and usage of opioids, narcotics, and other drugs. Many of the services provided at the school level were an extension of the community-wide need to address these issues. The district also worked with the local food bank and churches in the area to provide food, school supplies, and clothing.

Within the framework of creating a supportive culture, the district saw gains in moving the pendulum of students' performance in schools identified with students of high needs in the area of literacy and math. Leadership provided supports and opportunities for innovation, professional learning communities, focusing on Carol Dweck's work of *Growth Mindsets* and Malcolm Gladwell's *Outliers*.

Teachers fostered caring relationships with their students, demonstrated empathy for the challenges the student faced but never changed their resolve for high expectations. This was a necessary area to change educators' biases and beliefs about students' abilities through the incorporation of differentiated instruction, intentional accountability, and monitoring student progress.

Poverty and the constraints of a traditional system that lacks empathy for the changing needs of students can truly affect the quality of programs and the learning environment resulting in the perpetuation of underachievement. It was District 3's emphasis on the social-emotional development of the whole child that transformed the district's approach to curriculum, programs, decision-making, and accountability. It became the foundation on which everything rested upon.

Partnering with home, cognizant of grandparents serving as custodial parents, limited exposure to preschool or daycare, and other opportunities that would benefit the social and emotional development of the child, the district understood the importance of developing trusting relationships. This was done well at the school level, partnering with the home.

Setting goals for students within their success plans and discussing progress with families. Grade level standards and expectations were clear and shared with families and strategies to foster learning at home were shared. Schools were viewed as the extended family. Elementary and middle-school teachers set structure within the school day. Routines helped students to amalgamate into the school culture.

Principal and teacher relationships varied across the district, but at this level, there was strong coherence in high expectations and empathy. Principals were supportive to staff and worked along in identifying students in need of intervention and supports at each level. Central office and principal's relationships were professional in nature as a community of learners.

This was evident by team building and being supportive of one another's efforts in moving beyond comfort zone through innovation and risk taking.

The relationship between the superintendent and board of education was tangible. The superintendent helped the board of education realize the gaps that were present in the district. And that these gaps were socioeconomic in nature and a new generation of students was entering with pressing needs. The district was losing some families who opted for magnet schools in a neighboring urban city primarily due to the limited opportunities, and before and after school daycare.

Political tide for the district was economic, as they planned for the future. School enrollment was declining. A feasibility study showed the savings of consolidating schools; redistricting and reconfiguring grade construction would help in controlling the financial cost of educational programming in future years.

TPQ

1) Construct a theory of action for district improvement that addresses:
    a. Academic achievement gaps
    b. Building trusting and reciprocal relationships with stakeholders
    c. Equity and diversity

CHAPTER KEY IDEA

Addressing social-emotional needs first using a multilateral system of supports opens the doors to improved academic learning and closes the socioeconomic gap.

Chapter 20

Possibilities

> We are continually faced with a series of great opportunities brilliantly disguised as insoluble problems.
>
> —John W. Gardner

Leading unwanted change when change is needed is a herculean task for school superintendents. Inequities and injustices that prevail in the public education system for some children hinder their preparation to be competitive in a global world. Brokenness in our educational system as a result of strained relationships and failed reform efforts predicates itself on the essential need for trust among the strata of the educational hierarchy and the political arena.

Strong successful relationships require trust, respect for each other's roles, clear and distinct roles and responsibilities, a voice in the decision-making, and the emotional feeling of being valued. Each party should be viewed as a contributor to the relationship, resulting in shared and collaborative responsibility for the organization's mission, vision, goals, and outcomes.

SECTION 1: MOVING AWAY FROM TRADITIONALISM

Bureaucratic or the systemic institutionalization of education imposes unrelenting structures and requires fixed quotas of achievement. We have imposed levels of performance on ourselves and adjusted accordingly to make it appear that we are meeting those quotas. Expectation of students' academic performance becomes synonymous with demographic characteristics and false stereotypes that stigmatize our beliefs. Such stigmas result in low expectations or underachievement of students.

As a leader in a district, addressing the mindset and belief of staff concerning students' ability may be necessary, if there is a culture of low expectation. Changing this culture is a milestone. To change culture, the leader has to change the behaviors, beliefs, and customs that occur within the culture.

Districts struggle with issues of equity and diversity, especially around race and ethnicity, and social status. Breaking stereotypes of educators and community members alike, who may think of students of color and students from an impoverished background as lacking the ability to learn, is a challenge. It requires a mindset and heart change, going beyond tolerating the differences of another to embracing the difference. Wisdom would strategically use these differences to move the student academically forward through instructional practices that are culturally proficient and inclusive.

Reform efforts that try to push the needle to be more innovative and culturally responsive have only added more legislation, regulations, and training for educators. Some of these efforts have proven combative and have caused push back while others have removed a veil that masked how insensitive we have become. Without the proper prescription to address the issue, we cannot push forward.

Some policies, whether local, state, or federal, have lowered standards to a degree that it appears everyone is given an opportunity to achieve. It is a smokescreen as to what is truly occurring in schools. We see this within grading policies and practices: lowering the bar rather than setting higher standards and helping students achieve it. We have settled for mediocrity.

Retention policies have matriculated academically unprepared students, at the pretense of saving the student's emotional and psychological well-being and saving the district's profile. Statistically, numerous retentions feign poorly on a district. Perceptively, it looks as if the district is not doing its job, rather than blaming the performance of the student.

But we can ask, "What does not knowing how to read after graduating from high school do to the psyche?" or "What does it say about the education system that awarded a diploma to a student who cannot read?" A broken system has failed many of our children, throwing them away to only clear space for the next generation that the educational system may fail. Unfortunately, many districts are in this cycle that fails their children and community without any recompense or repentance. Yes, there are exceptions to the rule, but very few.

Bureaucratic traditionalism that we remain stuck in is manifested by practices and policies that tend to do more harm than good. We are fixated by the scheduled school day and year, the amount of time to be spent on each course, matriculating by chronological age as a gauge for completion, and fixed space for learning which is the school building.

Afraid to take the opportunity to break free from the routine, and status quo of traditionalism, we need to begin thinking outside the box for learning. That learning and instruction are more conducive to the needs of changing generations. The system as a whole may be left behind. Preference is to stick with the old tried system until it totally implodes, but traditionalism has rendered school districts ineffective in educating all students.

What is the dynamic change that must occur that releases the potential and possibility of better for our students? One option is clearly shifting from a traditionalist approach that is antediluvian in nature and perfunctory of the practices and policies that hold some of our children back: to a more forward-thinking approach that focuses on building cohesive relationships, personal approaches to student learning, addressing punitive mindsets that base ability on students' demographic condition, and preparing students to be globally competitive.

The best fill for a trench is to pack it to the degree that the ground is even for all students, which is equitable and adequate. Equity may be tipping the scales in an area in order to create balance in another. Providing what is needed for students to succeed such as personalization of learning and mastering fundamental skills is what could be the best fill for trenches.

Superintendents are constantly faced with addressing systemic problems and adapting in response to social pressures and issues occurring within the community. The surmounting task of leading a district forward almost seems impossible. But if we truly view adverse situations as opportunities rather than snares, there is always a glimmer of hope. This hope is in overcoming some of the challenges facing the educational system as a whole.

SECTION 2: IMPROVING RELATIONSHIPS THROUGH COMMUNICATION

Second, to keep focus on the children, superintendents must get to know the board members personally, their interests, goals, passions, and whether they have children in the district. The key to success is good communication through discussion and agreements with board members on each other's roles and responsibilities. Defining each other's roles will lend understanding when parties cross the boundaries of the relationship.

TEXTBOX 20.1

Cornerstones to Success

Serving on the board of education in a small, rural Connecticut town has been rewarding, sometimes frustrating, but most of all, a learning experience. Our district contains a single pK-8 elementary school, and our secondary school students have a choice of high schools in neighboring towns. In the past eight years, we have had four superintendents, three principals, and three directors of student services. This rate of turnover is not healthy for the district and as I reflect on the root causes, it really boils down to relationships and communication.

It is obvious that the relationship between the board chair and the superintendent is critical. However, the other interpersonal relationships between the board, administration, staff, and local town officials are just as important, if not more so, for an effective and productive school system.

As in any relationship, personal or business, trust and respect are the cornerstones of success. A superintendent who is transparent in dealing with the board and staff will earn their trust and support. They, in turn, will reflect this support to the community. When the board, administration, staff, and families are aligned, the school will flourish, and the students will prosper. Lack of respect, by any party, can quickly destroy this dynamic. I have witnessed both the devastating results of disrespect and the energizing optimism of trust and cooperation.

Respect does not mean silent agreement that may keep peace but does nothing to drive the continuous improvement for our schools that the schools so desperately need. Respect is the product of trust and the understanding of each person's roles and responsibilities. It requires frequent and effective communication.

The leaders of the various town boards need to keep each other informed and debate courteously while in public sessions. When the board of education trusts the superintendent and is respectful in public sessions, the superintendent can effectively execute the duties of running the district. Likewise, when the superintendent trusts the administration, they are more likely to trust the staff, and all can do their best work serving our children.

As the chairperson of the board, I often feel like a conductor—keeping all parties informed and building relationships. This part of the job has been the biggest learning experience. I learned patience, self-control, and humility. I also learned that most people are trustworthy and respectful when given the same courtesy. Some people never will be, and that is something I cannot control or change. Engaging the constructive people to create a critical mass of positive change to overcome the negative forces has been the greatest reward.

Jeanne Goulart
Board Member and Former Board Chair

Elections and the changing composition of the governance board have a significant effect on the relationship between the superintendent and the board of education. Each time new members join the board, there needs to be a renewed agreement and definition of roles.

Superintendents must be cognitively astute in understanding how to build relationships with board members. Balancing this relationship with understanding, stressing appreciation, and valuing their roles help to fortify the trust. It is important to have respect for the opinions of each individual board member and communicate with each one regarding their interests and goals for the district.

To improve communication, one should use planned priorities as a key to framing conversations. The best method of communication is direct and verbal conversation. Repetitiveness helps for ideas to sink in and also shows consistency. Superintendents should lead by example and display behavior that is consistent with the vision. When a behavior does not match the vision and there are inconsistencies, it overwhelms the receiver of information. Unaddressed inconsistencies undermine the credibility of communication.

Even when communication is clear and forthright, there is always the probability of someone questioning the communication. So, accept the casualties. Most misunderstandings are due to the lens through which one receives information. Deep conflicts are rooted in differences in beliefs, opinions, and perspectives.

A current example is the communication of information concerning Covid-19 and the SARS-CoV-2 virus. There is a great deal of misinformation, contradicting information, nonfactual information, and information that is of a conspirator nature that was emitted through the media. Information released by the media has caused questionable doubt in the ability of school leaders to make credible decisions concerning closures and quarantining practices.

When one fails to communicate the consensus of the majority and takes the risk of standing out, a leader will run the risk of being shamed and labeled a poor communicator. Also, the timing and release of information should be deliberate, helping to better make decisions for those who are affected.

Leaders by default will be blamed for any disruption to another's routine and inconvenience. But, it is necessary to make "good" decisions that benefit the well-being of the population in which you serve. Clarity, consistency, accepting responsibility for your contribution to the conflict, and acknowledging the loss are strategies for facilitating good communication.

Future leaders will need the fortitude to build cohesive relationships in order to make the change and to be a lens that magnifies the need for change and possibilities for improvement. By working together with all the layers of the hierarchical strata in tandem to provide a compass for the journey, improvement is certain. Strength of the relationship is determined by the trust that is forged and the desire to be successful as an organization.

Changing culture by changing behaviors will be a difficult task, especially changing adult behavior. Adults have years of habit forming experiences and innate beliefs that dictate their behaviors. Leaders may not necessarily change beliefs, but patterns of behavior can be addressed by habit forming practices; for instance, allowing children to choose their form of assessment for showing achievement of a learning objective. With such habit forming practices, behavior can be modified that results in a changed approach to how we perceive children's ability, instruct, interact with families, and engage within diverse environments.

SECTION 3: QUALITIES OF FUTURE LEADERS

Qualities of future leaders are not limited to relationship building and changing passive cultures but must also be forward thinkers and risk takers. Forward thinkers move outside of the familiar or traditional realm that fixates on systemic rules and rethinks how we do things and why. Approach to curriculum, instruction, assessment, and accountability should be cognoscente and respective of the individual educational needs of students preparing the learner to interact within a diverse environment.

Rather than thinking of students in mass, personalization should be the concern. Embedded within are twenty-first-century skills preparing students to be college and career ready and globally competitive.

Looking to the future of education, managing finances will continue to be a significant area that impacts schools. We see an upsurge in school funding from 2007 to 2015. Recessions and now a pandemic show a decline in school spending from 2016. Federal acts to give relief to the economy have also opened the door to a windfall of money coming to schools. Like all grants, funding comes with restrictions and limitations. Prior to this additional funding, districts with a high concentration of low-income families or low-wealth districts were highly impacted in funding. This resulted in teacher layoffs, increased class sizes, and reduced services.

What happens when the money to help the recovery of learning loss during the pandemic stops? Cities and towns will have many budgetary compromises and trade-offs to continue to support the educational system as it is currently managed. There will be discussions about re-prioritizing the programs offered and rescaling. Rethinking and adapting to new strategies as we did during Covid-19 and a new revived and vital usage of community partners and other outside resources. There will continue to be greater use of technology for the delivery of instruction.

TEXTBOX 20.2

School Budgets: What happens when the money to help the recovery of learning loss during the pandemic stops?

With the need for change, one may ask the question about sufficient financing to secure equitable, efficient, and accountable education for all children. Hopefully, states will address funding formulas to be transparent, equitable, and fully funded without stop gaps or levies, and to provide equity in the distribution of resources in a manner that those resources are identified. Potentially putting a cost differential in place to meet the needs of diverse learners. Both effective and efficient budgeting practices disburse resources in a manner that outputs improved achievement is the most equitable for all students.

Future leaders must plan for funding deficits after the surge of money coming into districts due to the American Rescue Relief Act ends. There will be a need for alternative strategies to budgeting and funding schools as we now know it. It will be necessary to project future costs of education by monitoring the community's economic growth and demographic projections, educational parameters of enrollment rates, student flows, class size, and teacher-to-student ratio.

Forward thinkers must be willing to take the innovative risk that stands out from the norm. It also requires bringing all the stakeholders with you! Strategically planning for change so that it is sustainable and any successor can build from it.

Leadership's forwardness, willingness, and adaptability to forge through obstacles that are hindrances are necessary for effective and transformative school districts. Viewing these obstacles as opportunities rather than constraints could effectively shift the trajectory of leadership within school districts and the educational system as a whole.

TEXTBOX 20.3

Leadership and Relationships

Leadership has many faces: that of an instructional leader, a manager, a facilitator, but that role can change in every area of the workplace depending on circumstances that may occur. My personal leadership style is one of no excuses and one that is collaborative in nature.

I am an instructional leader who believes in sharing decisions and working collaboratively with staff, students, parents, and all other stakeholders in the community. It is about forming an inner circle, composed of those key stakeholders, and identifying the key people who would be willing to work on school improvement and to influence others to join us in ensuring that all students are represented.

As an administrator (principal, central office administrator, and/or superintendent of schools) you need to assess the needs of the district as it relates to student growth and achievement, and organize that data to support your findings and present it to all to garner buy-in. This is a part of developing your strategic plan. Throughout the process, key individuals who have a clear understanding of the vision need to assist you in moving the agenda forward. While embarking on this process, when resistance became evident by one of the members from the stakeholder group, the other stakeholders became a positive influence for those in doubt.

Involving parents and asking them for their input are essential in the delivery of the vision for the community at large. Lack of coherence within the inner circle can cause a division. This is an example of how trenches can form and become a problem if you are not aware of the school community's needs. For this to happen, I had to be flexible, but at the same time consistent in my belief that all students can learn. In order to achieve this with staff, I had to create a level of trust (reciprocal) to create teams that could work together to ensure all students could reach their potential.

As I read the preliminary chapters for this book, the role that superintendents play in school districts and the variety of metaphors that were discussed in each chapter were evident in the role I played in the districts I served. As I think back to my leadership as a superintendent of schools, I realize that I dealt with the trenches and the cisterns that affect the districts and the children we served. Trenches kept adults and students from moving forward to support student growth, and cisterns maintained students in situations where the system kept them from growing academically and emotionally.

As an administrator and as a superintendent of schools, the trenches could be in the way only if you do not see what is broken and how to repair it. Upon entry into a district, it is important to develop an entry plan that identifies the needs specific to the community you are serving.

I also dealt with the many cisterns that were not any different than they were back in the day when students' parents were themselves in schools as students. For instance, the importance of providing a full-day kindergarten program versus half-day, some stakeholders struggled to understand the importance of this. Why change it? It worked for me and when my children went to school. Even many staff members found themselves as not being able to accept the changes coming, such as the inclusion of all students in all aspects of their education.

As a leader, I have hope for the future of all of the constituents we serve so that everyone can reach his/her potential in our schools without all the impediments we face every day as school leaders. I am optimistic that change is always difficult but possible if we believe it can happen. We need to continue to take risks to ensure that all students succeed. If the risk benefits children, then just do it!

Ana V. Ortiz
Retired Superintendent
Past President of Association of Latino
Administrators and Superintendents

SECTION 4: REVELATION IN THE METAPHORS

What is impossible can possibly be addressed with the right strategies, renewed vision and outlook, structural changes in the educational system, behaviors and attitudes, and fidelity. The future of the educational system is contingent upon the response to past traditions and forced reactions of change to current conditions. For example, new models of learning were forged in response to addressing the needs of remote learning.

Strongholds and obstacles that have effected student achievement and educational reform still continue to exist and potentially exacerbated during the Covid-19 pandemic. Visually, the metaphors have created perspectives of what nets create that are strongholds in the system that are no longer working or have not worked for many generations.

Broken relationships among stakeholders have created trenches, creating an even greater expanse of division and incoherence in vision and mission. Instability and unsustainability have weakened the foundation of the educational system and weakened the outputs that we desire to see in our children that are preparing them for the future. Failing to prepare our children for a future world drains our workforce and competitive global edge.

These metaphors revealed what is pervasively true. They also show hidden deception of the intent to do right, which further creates deeper harm to children. Leaders of today and the future cannot overlook the deeper calls for equity and justice and what this means without losing democratic processes or erasing history. But rather, this deeper call recontextualizes history and traditions to catapult us into a new age that learned from its past, not disregard the past.

Recognizing the importance of relationships, leaders will have to overcome their own character flaws when building trusting relationships. Also, the leaders should learn to relinquish some of their "ego" to survive the judgmental pious culture in which the world finds itself. Good leaders have a servant heart that appreciates the value of others and realize that they are not above any job.

Leaders are the keepers of stability and fulfillers of the social-emotional needs of both students and staff. Even in our rediscovery of how to fit an old model into new technology, the school day's schedule in regard to parents' work life and the school staff adapting new requirements of work and balancing their personal life added new stressors to the workings of the educational system.

We have a new paradigm shift of purpose. However, the functionality of preparing students to interact in society remains the same. Indoctrination of the swing or direction the society is moving, so that students conform, is still the larger goal of the educational system. We want students to be productive, creative, and politically correct in moral standards within the framework established by the pervasive culture of the day.

And as we look to the future of schooling, marking this decade as a pivotal opportunity for change, what can we imagine? Do we have the cognitive capacity to address the root of the problem? What do we believe? Can we remove the snares that are hidden and in plain view that spring up catching one unawares? Those that have been conditioned for so long are deadened to the response and unassuming as if it is a matter of fact.

We see numerous obstacles bear on the present state of the educational system as an institution. We can no longer take these strongholds as circumspection but credible facts of moral imperatives. Exposing such entrapping and our response to these strongholds should indeed cause pressure all around, preempting change.

The structure and strongholds of the educational system have almost dullened our senses to its effects on our children. It has desensitized us, created commonality, and made commonplace the occurrence of such obstacles that we fail to fight for a better way. The intent of the educational system was not to suppress or even oppress, but to liberate. Somehow the system has become a snare to itself, contradictory to its original purpose; a design flaw that has a larger negative impact.

Conceiver of falsehoods digs pits for others to fall into. The conceiver becomes the victim of his own destructive plan. Malignant devices result in their own ruin. When allowed to run their course, things that are not just will destroy themselves. Both the forward-thinking leader and the community they serve must be willing to open the nets, fill in the trenches, stable the foundation to prevent sinkholes, and refill the cisterns, metaphorically speaking. Working within the confines of the current system is not for the faint of heart!

TPQ

1) What is the dynamic change that must occur that releases the potential and possibility of better for students?
2) Why is communication a pivotal component to change? Design a communication plan:
    a. First assess and audit your current practices
    b. Decide on the best approach/methods to sharing information with your stakeholders
    c. Determine timeframe and time management for communication
    d. Monitor the results of communication; reassess and look for ways to improve
3) To be a forward-thinking leader, what will you need in your toolbox to open up nets? Fill trenches? Stabilize the foundation to prevent sinkholes and refill the cisterns with employable students?

CHAPTER KEY IDEAS

1. Many times, the expectation of students' academic performance is driven by demographic characteristics and stereotypes that stigmatize beliefs.
2. Invoking change may require a reset of the current culture. To change the culture of a district requires a change in behaviors, beliefs, and practices.
3. The dynamic change that needs to occur in the education system to shift from tradition to a forward-thinking approach is directed to addressing these areas: relationship building, personalization of learning, removal of stereotypes and stigmas, and preparation of students to compete globally.
4. Trust and communication through discussion and agreements of roles and responsibilities help to establish a cohesive relationship.
5. Future leaders must be willing to move outside of the familiar or traditional realm and rethink the approach of how we do things in education.

Bibliography

CHAPTER 1

Cuban, Larry. "Standards Versus Customization Finding the Balance." *Educational Leadership* 69, no. 5 (2012):10–15.

CHAPTER 4

Bonner, Portia. *The Influence of Secondary Science Teachers' Pedagogical Content Knowledge, Educational Beliefs and Perceptions of the Curriculum on Implementation and Science Reform.* Dissertation: University of Connecticut, 2001.
Gabriel, John. *How to Thrive As a Teacher Leader.* Virginia: Association for Supervision and Curriculum Development, 2005.
Jackson, Yvette. *The Pedagogy of Confidence.* New York: Columbia University Teachers College Press, 2011.
National Urban Alliance. *Briefing Notebook.* New York: Columbia University Teachers College, 1999.

CHAPTER 5

Bryk, Anthony and Barbara Schneider. *Trust in Schools.* New York: Russell Sage, 2002.
Kimball, Dale. "The Cornerstone Relationship Between CEO and Board President." *The School Administrator* 62, no. 1 (2005):6.
National School Boards Association. *Do School Boards Matter?* American School Board Journal, December 2002.

Pandiscio, Herbert. *A Power Shift in Public Education*. New York: Rowman & Littlefield Education, 2009.

Papke, Edgar. *The Elephant in the Boardroom*. New Jersey: Career Press, 2016.

CHAPTER 6

Chubb, John and Terry Moe. *Politics, Markets & America's Schools*. Washington, D.C.: Brookings Institution, 1990.

Jehl, Jeanne, Martin Blank and Barbara McCloud. *Education and Community Building*. Washington, D.C.: Institute of Educational Leadership, 2001.

Lindahl, Ronald. *The Role of Organizational Climate and Culture in the School Improvement Process: A Review of the Knowledge Base*. Texas: Rice University – Openstax, 2011.

Maslow, A. H. *Motivation and Personality*. New York: Harper & Row, 1954.

CHAPTER 8

Levenson, Nathan, Karla Baehr, James Smith and Claire Sullivan. *Spending Money Wisely: Getting the Most from School District Budgets*. District Management Council, 2014.

CHAPTER 9

Koretz, Daniel. *The Testing Charade*. Chicago: The University of Chicago Press, 2017.

Lambert, Linda. *Leadership Capacity for Lasting School Improvement*. Virginia: Association for Supervision and Curriculum Development, 2003.

Zmuda, Allison, Greg Curtis and Diane Ullman. *Learning Personalized*. California: Jossey-Bass, 2015.

CHAPTER 10

Koretz, Daniel. *The Testing Charade*. Chicago: The University of Chicago Press, 2017.

Vollmere, Jamie. *Schools Cannot Do It Alone*. Iowa: Enlightenment Press, 2010.

CHAPTER 11

Zoukis, Christopher. "Basic Literacy A Crucial Tool to Stem School to Prison Pipeline." *Huffpost*: www.Huffpost.com, 2017.

CHAPTER 16

Bennis, Warren and Robert Thomas. *Crucibles of Leadership*. Harvard Business Review. https://hbr.org/2002/09/crucibles-of-leadership

CHAPTER 17

Lindsey, Randall, Laraine M. Roberts and Franklin CampbellJones. *The Culturally Proficient School*. California: Corwin Press, 2005.
Lindsey, Randall, KiKanza Nuri-Robins, Raymond D. Terrell and Delores B. Lindsey. *Cultural Proficiency*. California: Corwin Press, 2018.
Singleton, Glenn. *Courageous Conversations About Race*. California: Corwin Press, 2006, 2014.

About the Author

Portia S. Bonner, PhD, is a veteran educator serving over the span of thirty years. Currently, she is working as a consultant to school districts to assist with systemic improvement. She has served in multiple capacities in education from school teacher to superintendent of schools. As an agent of change, she has assisted underperforming schools and districts in their directional focus of improvement and building partnerships with their community.